The Artful Pie

Unforgettable recipes for creative cooks

By
Lisa Cherkasky
and Renée Comet

CHAPTERS™

CHAPTERS PUBLISHING LTD., SHELBURNE, VERMONT 05482

To Marty, our favorite computer wizard, and to George, who prefers cake

Published by
Chapters Publishing Ltd.
2031 Shelburne Road
Shelburne, Vermont 05482

Library of Congress Cataloging-in-Publication Data
Cherkasky, Lisa
    The artful pie: unforgettable recipes for creative cooks
        by Lisa Cherkasky and Renée Comet
        p.   cm.
    ISBN 1-881527-16-6 (hardcover) ISBN 1-57630-022-6 (paperback)
        1. Pies.   I. Comet, Renée   II. Title.
    TX773.C5218   1993
    641.8'652—dc20   93-9894

Printed and bound in Canada by
Friesen Printers
Altona, Manitoba

Concept by Lisa Cherkasky and Renée Comet
Book Design by Hans Teensma / Impress, Inc., Northampton, Massachusetts

Cover photograph: Cool Lime Pie With Tequila
Art by Janice Olson. Recipe on page 58.

Acknowledgments

THE AUTHORS wish to thank all the people who patiently, diligently and generously helped us with this book. Without the wonderful and wildly varying creativity of the artists who contributed work, it would not exist.

Recipes or recipe inspiration came from Peter Brett, Joan Lynch, Elsie Schroeder, Betty Lou Skutley, Barbara Stratton, Kay Strutz, Susan Stuck and Hélène Uzan.

Thanks also to Clare Cherkasky, Sally Collins, Les Dames D'Escoffier, Lisa Ekus, Amanda Manheim, Blaine Marshall and Stuart Rombro for their encouragement and good advice, and to Amy Pastan and Mary Lynn Skutley for their impeccable guidance.

We also wish to express our gratitude to all the friends who happily tested and tasted pies for us, especially John Archambeault, Susan Dirk, Ralph Eubanks, Elizabeth Eberhardt, Françoise Evans, Judy Gerber, Ruth Gresser, Jo Hodgin, Linda Komes, Jerry Lynch, Holly Moskerintz, Carol Rest, Deborah Rivers, Peggy Schlegel, Leila Smith, Gary Sutto, Kathy Swekel, Cathy Tyson, Norrene Vogt and Donna Workman. Diane Koss, Melissa McClelland and Evie Righter provided valuable insight and attention to detail. And finally, thank you, Deanna D'Errico, for the use of your chair.

We are grateful to all our parents who instilled in us a strong work ethic. A special mention goes to our mothers: Jeanne Comet, who is too impatient to make pie, and Shirley Cherkasky for her belief that the only food not improved by whipped cream is sauerkraut.

Last, thank you to the designer of this book, Hans Teensma of Impress, Inc., his assistant, Jeff Potter, and to all those at Chapters Publishing: Rux Martin, Barry Estabrook, James Lawrence, Alice Lawrence and Deidre Stapleton.

Contents

The Artful Pie

Strawberry-Orange Frappe Pie	40	Sour Cherries in Gewürztraminer Pie	100
Lemon-Lime Slice Pie	44	Ricotta Nut Crunch Pie	104
Backyard Green Tomato Pie	48	Butter-Brickle Banana Cream Pie	108
Fresh Peach Pie	52	Peach Pie, Oklahoma Style	112
Cool Lime Pie With Tequila	56	Upside-Down Fried-Pear Pie	116
Apple Butter Apple Pie	60	Strawberry Jam Pie	120
Eat-Me-Quick Buttermilk Custard Pie	64	Black Bottom Pie	124
Mom's Lemon Meringue Pie	68	Tutti-Frutti Pie	128
Ultrasmooth Chocolate Malted Pie	72	Raspberry-Rhubarbara Pie	132
Apricot and White Cherry Pie	76	Nutty Coconut Cream Pie	136
Summer Berry Chiffon Pie	80	Chocolate Caramel Hazelnut Pie	140
Very Berry Pie	84	Tiny Chess Pies	144
Brandied Butterscotch Pie	88	Minnesota Gooseberry Pie	148
Bourbon-Spiked Pecan Pie	92	Brown Sugar Apple Crumb Pie	152
Mocha Fudge Pie	96	Peppery Sweet Potato Pie	156

Introduction

In a sense, my preparation as a pie baker began well before I was born. I discovered this while riding along on a city bus with my 80-year-old grandmother when, out of the blue, she began to tell me the story of the 14,000 pies she had baked between the years of 1933 and 1937, six days a week, between 4:00 and 7:00 A.M.

During the early years of their marriage, my grandfather drove a truck for the Dependon bakery selling breads, rolls, doughnuts and cheesecake on commission. Dependon offered pies as well, but their commercial pies "just didn't move." It was the Depression, and to earn extra money, my grandmother decided to bake the pies herself. My grandfather added her homemade goods to his line, and at 25 cents apiece, they were very popular. Each day he delivered the ordered pies—lattice-topped cherry or blueberry, lemon custard, apple or pumpkin, and chocolate, pineapple or coconut cream—and each day he picked up the empty pie tins to be filled again the following morning.

My grandmother is a woman of few words. That story probably tripled the information I knew about her younger years. I was eager for more. What other kinds of pie did she make? Which was her favorite? What sort of fat did she use in the crust? How could she bake that many pies?

"You get up early," she replied.

Apparently, there is no escaping family destiny when it comes to pie baking. Mastering pie dough was a required course in my mother's kitchen. A tender crust was paramount. After her explanation, I could picture each particle of butter trapped between paper-thin layers of flour, creating a dough that could be gently and quickly worked into submission—fragile, flaky and with a faint edge of saltiness.

I began baking for my family and friends, using my mother's recipes. But pie making, I soon learned, lends itself to almost infinite variety. The seasons, the refrigerator and the cook's appetite and imagination all create inspiration and set boundaries. At once impressive and unremarkable, pie can be complicated and challenging or simple and homey. Whether ordinary or elegant, though, a pie is not something to eat by yourself. It should be made to share, preferably while fresh and warm.

This project grew out of a six-year collaboration between me, a cook and food stylist, and Renée Comet, a food photographer. We suspected that there were certain aesthetic and creative elements that food and art share, and we had an idea: to do a book of original recipes photographed on original works of art commissioned specifically for the occasion. What better subject for such a tribute than pie?

Explaining our idea to artists was not as simple as we had expected. We told them that they were free to work in the medium of their choice as long as they produced a two-dimensional horizontal piece, 26 inches long and 13 inches wide. It should be a single continuous image that would be split into two squares by the binding of the book. We also asked them to make sure the art included a lifesize plate on which we would place a slice of pie.

The response was enthusiastic, and before too long we had commitments from 36 artists. Shortly thereafter, Washington, D.C. artist Craig Cahoon arrived with his painting. By coincidence, I had brought in a pie for tasting. He had painted a desert scene: a cactus, a skull and a seemingly endless sky. My pie was Lemon-Lime Slice, a pale citrus filling with a crust the color of beautiful brown sand. I cut a wedge and laid it down on the painting. Renée added light to simulate direct desert sun. This casual test—a combination of serendipity and contrivance—produced a photograph that became final. It appears on page 44.

Several months passed, during which I baked pie after pie, and a collection of wildly varied art was completed and delivered. The range of media was remarkable: pencil, plaster, watercolor, woodcut, sawdust, oil, acrylic, broken glass, oil pastel and jellybeans.

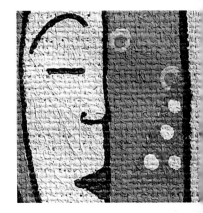

As the photography progressed, we added three-dimensional props or special effects to some of the sets. Mom's Lemon Meringue Pie on Rebecca Wood's bright watercolor (page 68) is accompanied by a painted cup of tea with real steam wafting from it. Elyse Shalom's acrylic on burlap (page 96) depicts a pair of grinning utensils, their arms surrounding Mocha Fudge Pie on a painted plate. Across the page, a real drinking glass lies tipped on its side, chocolate milk splashing out. We placed glass bubbles on Gerry Wyche's painted pond (page 148), where Minnesota Gooseberry Pie floats on a lilypad.

Although we carefully matched pies with art and planned each page meticulously, the photography took much of its life from details we could not control: coincidence and happy accident. One afternoon we were photographing Fresh Peach Pie on a beautiful summer-lit oil pastel by Micki Kirk. Renée had brought in a branch of new peach leaves. All the parts of the composition were in place—art, pie, props and lighting—when it struck me that we were missing something. How about putting a ladybug on a leaf? As a matter of fact, Renée had seen one in the studio the day before. That polka-dotted guest couldn't have made a more timely appearance and is captured on page 52.

Through all our efforts, intentional or intuitive, calculated or impulsive, pie remained the focus of our attention. At least one perfect, delicious slice was always front and center, around which spun art, light and props.

As appealing as these pies look, taste ultimately determined whether or not they would be included. Some of the recipes are strictly traditional. Mom's Lemon Meringue Pie is my mother's prize-winning recipe. Black Bottom Pie re-creates the sought-after specialty of a Wisconsin chef. Betty Lou's Rhubarb Pie comes straight from the recipe files of a friend's mother; I like it because it has not been touched by modern "liteness." My cousin's old-fashioned Fresh Peach Pie is simply spiced with nutmeg.

Other pies, however, present twists on time-honored recipes, the result of play between the traditional and the personal. Cool Lime Pie With Tequila, Nutty Coconut Cream Pie, Ultrasmooth Chocolate Malted Pie, Butter-Brickle Banana Cream Pie and Sour Cherries in Gewürztraminer Pie all owe their inspiration to various resources: cupboard, market or

collective unconscious.

By their nature, many pie recipes are seasonal and rely on the availability and peak flavor of fruit. Canned or frozen fruit usually does not do the cook justice. The beauty of much good baking is the short season of its players, and a large part of sensual pleasure is in the anticipation. For times when you are without fresh fruit, there is always the richness of nuts, chocolate, dried fruits, butter and cream.

A synthesis of creativity and imagination in many forms, **The Artful Pie** has been an edible and visual puzzle on several levels: two-dimensional in the artwork and photography, three-dimensional in the kitchen and the studio, gustatory on the plate and palate, and scientific in the baking.

Although at first glance this is a book for looking, it is clearly a cooking book too. We hope that you will keep it near your rolling pin and pie plates, and that you will use it.

Of course, the final touch to every page is missing: a smudge, smear or drip deftly added in your own kitchen.

—*Lisa Cherkasky*

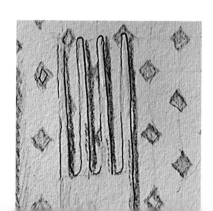

Pie Crust Recipes

BASIC PIE DOUGH FOR A SINGLE-CRUST PIE

2   **cups all-purpose flour**

¾   **teaspoon salt**

10 **tablespoons very cold, unsalted butter, vegetable shortening or lard, or a combination, cut into small pieces**

5–6 **tablespoons very cold water**

Follow instructions for Mixing Pie Dough (page 11).
Makes enough for a 9- or 10-inch single crust.

BASIC PIE DOUGH FOR A DOUBLE-CRUST PIE

3   **cups all-purpose flour**

1   **teaspoon salt**

1   **cup very cold, unsalted butter, vegetable shortening or lard, or a combination, cut into small pieces**

8–10 **tablespoons very cold water**

Follow instructions for Mixing Pie Dough (page 11).
Makes enough for a 9- or 10-inch double crust or two 9-inch single crusts.

BUTTER, LARD OR VEGETABLE SHORTENING?

Use **butter** for a crust with a delicate taste but a harder, less fragile texture than a crust made with vegetable shortening or lard. The flavor of butter is especially appropriate for nut, cream, custard and chiffon pies. For the best of both worlds, replace one-third to one-half of the butter with vegetable shortening; your pastry will be crisp *and* buttery.

Use **solid vegetable shortening** for a crisp crust. Shortening imparts almost no flavor of its own but makes a dough that is less fragile and easier to roll than a dough made with lard. I prefer a crust that uses both shortening, for ease in handling and rolling, and another fat, such as butter or lard.

Although many people have reservations about eating **lard**, there is no replacing it when it comes to good old-fashioned, melt-in-your-mouth flakiness. Lard is particularly suited to double-crust, fruit-filled pies. Because pie dough made entirely with lard can be frustrating to handle and roll and a little strong in flavor, it is a good idea to replace one-third to one-half of the lard with vegetable shortening or butter.

Lard is usually found in the dairy case, and it will

appeal to the frugal. Use what you need, and then store the remainder in the freezer, well wrapped.

FLAKY CITRUS PASTRY

FLAKY CITRUS PASTRY is the dough of choice for Apricot and White Cherry Pie, but it would also go well with Minnesota Gooseberry Pie, Mom's Lemon Meringue Pie, Tutti-Frutti Pie or Betty Lou's Rhubarb Pie.

3   cups all-purpose flour
1   teaspoon salt
½   teaspoon sugar
1   tablespoon grated lemon zest
1   teaspoon grated orange zest
1   cup very cold, unsalted butter or ½ cup very cold, unsalted butter plus ½ cup very cold vegetable shortening, cut into small pieces
6–7   tablespoons very cold water

Follow instructions for Mixing Pie Dough (page 11), adding the sugar, lemon zest and orange zest to the flour and salt. *Makes enough for a 9- or 10-inch double crust.*

CORNMEAL PASTRY

CORNMEAL PASTRY is recommended for Susan's Unbaked Blueberry Pie. Its crunch is a pleasing surprise.

1   cup plus 5 tablespoons all-purpose flour
3   tablespoons yellow cornmeal
¼   teaspoon salt
½   cup very cold, unsalted butter, cut into small pieces
3–4   tablespoons very cold water

Follow instructions for Mixing Pie Dough (page 11), adding the cornmeal to the flour and salt. *Makes enough for a 9- or 10-inch single crust.*

COCOA PASTRY

CHOCOLATE LOVERS will appreciate the little extra effort needed to make Cocoa Pastry. Use this dough for Mocha Fudge Pie, Chocolate Caramel Hazelnut Pie or Summer Berry Chiffon Pie.

1   cup plus 5 tablespoons all-purpose flour
2   tablespoons unsweetened cocoa powder
2   teaspoons sugar
¼   teaspoon salt
½   cup very cold unsalted butter, cut into small pieces
3–4   tablespoons very cold water

Follow instructions for Mixing Pie Dough (page 11), adding the cocoa powder and sugar to the flour and salt. *Makes enough for a 9- or 10-inch single crust.*

Pie Crust Basics

BEAR IN MIND that your pie does not have to be "perfect." Food is, after all, organic. Each time you prepare it, the same recipe will undoubtedly produce a slightly (or greatly) different result. Fruits vary from harvest to harvest in their sweetness, juiciness, texture, size and taste, to name a few possibilities. Flour and butter will not give absolutely consistent results, even if you stick to the same brands. A humid day or a very warm kitchen will affect the chemistry of your pastry. When baking, try to measure as accurately as possible, but remember that we are all victims—often happy ones—of the weather, the grocer and our moods.

MIXING PIE DOUGH

TO BAKE A SUCCESSFUL PIE with a tender crust, it is helpful to keep in mind that pie dough is made up of many small particles of fat surrounded by layers of flour. When the dough is baked, the fat melts and creates flaky pockets. It is imperative that your ingredients start out cold and remain as cold as possible. Remember that warmed fat will blend too easily with the flour, the layers will disappear, and you will be left with a disappointingly tough crust.

Handle pie dough no more than necessary. Most people are aware that bread dough requires kneading, which gives the dough structure, allowing it to rise properly and have a chewy texture. With pie dough, your objective is just the opposite; you do not want your pastry to be strong and chewy. The less you work the dough, the more fragile and flaky your crust will be. Don't worry if your dough does not look absolutely smooth and flawless; once it is rolled, crimped and baked, it will be lovely.

By hand: In a medium mixing bowl, stir together the flour and salt. Add the cold fat to the flour all at once. Working quickly with a pastry blender or two table knives, cut the fat into the flour until the mixture resembles coarse bread crumbs. (You may also rub the fat into the flour with your fingertips, but if you do, you must work especially quickly to avoid warming the fat.)

Sprinkle the water over the flour and, using a fork or wooden spoon, bring the dough together with a few quick strokes. If the dough is too dry or crumbly, sprinkle in a little more water and then stir it in. With your hands, knead the dough several times—just enough to form it into a ball. If you have made enough

11

dough for 2 single-crust pies, divide the dough into 2 equal pieces. If it is for a double-crust pie, divide the dough into 2 slightly unequal pieces. (The larger piece will be used for the bottom crust.) Flatten the dough into a smooth disk (or disks), wrap it securely in plastic and refrigerate for at least 20 minutes.

In the food processor: Fit the steel blade into the bowl of the food processor. Put the flour and salt into the bowl and pulse to combine them. Add the cold fat all at once and pulse until the mixture resembles coarse bread crumbs.

Sprinkle the water over the flour and pulse until a dough begins to form. Test the texture of the dough with your fingers. If it is too dry or crumbly, sprinkle in a little more water and pulse for a few seconds to combine.

Turn the dough out onto the counter and, with your hands, knead it just enough to form a ball. If you have made enough dough for 2 single-crust pies, divide the dough into 2 equal pieces. If it is for a double-crust pie, divide the dough into 2 slightly unequal pieces. (The larger piece will be used for the bottom crust.) Flatten the dough into a smooth disk (or disks), wrap it securely in plastic and refrigerate for at least 20 minutes.

With an electric mixer: Fit the electric mixer with the paddle. (If your mixer does not have a paddle, mix the dough by hand or in the food processor.) Put the flour and salt into the mixing bowl and on low speed, stir to combine. Add the cold fat all at once and blend on medium-low speed until the mixture resembles coarse bread crumbs.

Sprinkle the water over the flour and blend on low speed just until a dough begins to form. Test the texture of the dough with your fingers. If it is too dry or crumbly, sprinkle in a little more water and mix briefly on low speed to combine.

Turn the dough out onto the counter and, with your hands, knead it just enough to form a ball. If you have made enough dough for 2 single-crust pies, divide the dough into 2 equal pieces. If it is for a double-crust pie, divide the dough into 2 slightly unequal pieces. (The larger piece will be used for the bottom crust.) Flatten the dough into a smooth disk (or disks), wrap it securely in plastic and refrigerate for at least 20 minutes.

A FEW THINGS TO KEEP IN MIND WHEN MIXING DOUGH:

- ❧ Work quickly and use a light touch.
- ❧ Use cold ingredients.
- ❧ Keep the dough as cold as possible while mixing it to prevent the fat from becoming soft. If your hands are warm, a quick rinse under cold water will cool them down.
- ❧ Add only as much liquid as is needed to form a smooth dough. The addition of too much liquid will produce soggy, tough pastry.
- ❧ Mix the dough just enough to hold it together and no more. If the flour and fat are too thoroughly amalgamated, the dough will be tough.

ROLLING PIE DOUGH

Before you begin: Many of the guidelines that apply to

mixing pie dough will steer you past the pitfalls of dough rolling as well. In addition to the methods mentioned above—working quickly and keeping the dough as cold as possible—there are a few other suggestions to heed. Dough that is overworked or rolled with too much force will become elastic and inevitably spring back when it is baked. A prebaked pie shell that shrinks will be too small to accommodate the filling. To prevent shrinking, give your dough some time in the refrigerator, at least 20 minutes and up to an hour, before and after rolling. Chilling also firms the fat in the dough, ensuring flakiness.

Rolling: Remove the chilled dough from the refrigerator 5 to 10 minutes before rolling. If, after sitting at room temperature, the dough is still too hard to roll, work it gently with your fingertips until it softens slightly. Be careful not to overdo it. If making a double-crust pie, roll out the larger piece first.

Give the work surface a light sprinkling of flour and set the dough down on it. Sprinkle a little flour over the top of the dough and rub some flour onto the rolling pin. Working from the center out, roll the dough into a circle, lifting the edges occasionally to loosen them. If necessary, to prevent sticking, add a little flour underneath as you lift the dough. Occasionally, between rolls, lift the dough and give it a half turn. Use an empty pie pan as a guide for size by holding it over the circle of dough. The circle is big enough when it extends 2 inches beyond the edge of the pie pan.

To lift the dough into the pie pan, first fold it in half. (If your dough sticks to the counter, use a thin metal spatula to release it.) Fold the dough again, into quarters. Position the dough in the pie pan by setting the point of the pastry in the center of the pan. Unfold the dough and fit it smoothly into the pan. With scissors or a small knife, trim the edges, leaving a 1-inch overhang. Save the trimmings. If there are any holes or cracks in the dough, use the scraps to patch them by firmly pressing a small piece of dough over the hole. A single-crust pie shell is now ready for crimping. Refrigerate the bottom of a double-crust pie shell for 20 minutes before filling, covering with a top crust, and crimping.

Tip: Rolling pie dough out on wax paper will prevent it from sticking to the counter. To do this, cut a large piece of wax paper and moisten one side with a damp sponge. Stick the moistened side of the paper onto the counter. Lightly flour the top of the paper just as you would if you were rolling the dough directly on the counter. After rolling the dough, lift the paper by its corners, invert the dough into the pie pan and peel off the paper.

A FEW THINGS TO KEEP IN MIND WHEN ROLLING DOUGH:

∾ Always allow the dough to rest in the refrigerator before and after rolling. Don't rush the dough; this is definitely a case where haste makes waste.

∾ Work as quickly as possible to avoid warming the dough any more than absolutely necessary.

∾ Use enough flour to prevent sticking, but do not overdo it. Too much will dry and toughen the dough.

~ Always roll from the center out, applying pressure evenly. The dough should spread easily in front of the pin. The idea is to allow the dough to *spread*, not *stretch*. Dough that is forced to stretch will shrink when baked.

~ Avoid rerolling; it toughens the dough.

CRIMPING PIE CRUST

CRIMPING SERVES to take up the slack in the edge of the pie shell and to decorate the pie. A single crust is crimped before it is chilled. A double crust is crimped after the top crust has been set in place. There are many ways to crimp a pie crust; the method you choose is purely personal. A basic fluted edge is accomplished by pressing the edge of the dough in toward the center of the pie with your left index finger, while pushing the dough *out* (around your left index finger) with your right thumb and index finger. Repeat all the way around the edge of the pie. After crimping, refrigerate a single-crust pie for 20 minutes before prebaking or filling.

ADDING A TOP CRUST

ROLL THE TOP CRUST just as you did the bottom. Use an empty pie pan as a guide for size by holding it over the circle of dough. The circle is big enough when it extends ½ inch beyond the edge of the pie pan. Fill the pie and lay the top crust over the filling. With scissors or a small knife, trim the top crust to ½ inch beyond the edge of the filling. Fold the edge of the bottom crust in over the edge of the top crust and press firmly with your fingertips to seal the seam.

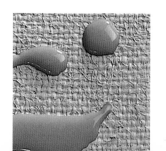

Crimp the edge. With a small, sharp knife, cut 5 to 6 slits in the top crust to allow the steam to escape. If you plan to brush the top crust with a glaze or egg wash, cut the slits *after* you have applied the glaze. It is not necessary to allow the top crust to rest before baking.

STORING PIE DOUGH

PIE DOUGH, well wrapped, may be stored in the refrigerator for up to 2 days. A pie crust that has been rolled and fitted into a pie pan will stay fresh in the freezer for up to 2 months. If you wish to freeze more than one pie crust, cover each one with a sheet of wax paper and stack them carefully. Wrap pie crusts destined for the freezer in at least two well-sealed layers of plastic wrap. Frozen pie crusts do not need to be thawed before they are filled or baked.

PREBAKING PIE SHELLS

PREBAKING A single-crust pie shell, also called blind baking, ensures a crisp crust. Generally, prebaking is for cream, custard or fruit-filled pies that will not be baked again once they are filled. Occasionally, a recipe in this book calls for prebaking a crust that will be baked again after filling. Prebaking helps to prevent the crust from absorbing the moisture in the filling and becoming soggy.

For best results, bake your crust in a glass pie pan in the lower third of the oven.

Preheat the oven to 425 degrees F. Remove the chilled shell from the refrigerator and line it with a square of aluminum foil or parchment paper. Fill the lined shell with about 1½ cups baking weights, dried beans or rice (I have also used small pasta). Bake the crust until the edge just begins to color, about 8 minutes. Remove from the oven and carefully lift out the foil. Prick the bottom and sides of the crust with a fork and then return it to the oven. If you will be using the crust for a pie that will be filled and baked again, bake the crust only until it is partially done and golden brown, about 8 minutes more. If you plan to use the crust for a pie that will not be baked again, bake the crust completely, until it is well browned (I particularly like the taste of a well-browned crust for nut-filled pies), about 12 to 14 minutes more. Check the crust often as it bakes. If the bottom or sides begin to puff, prick them lightly with a fork. If necessary, deflate any puffing by pressing the crust gently with a paper towel or tea towel. If the edge of the crust is browning too quickly, cover it with strips of aluminum foil.

If any holes or cracks form as the crust bakes, use scraps of dough to patch them. Affix the raw dough to the crust with a dab of cold water. Return the crust to the oven for a few minutes to bake and seal the patches.

Baking Tip: Do not put a hot filling into a cold crust or the crust will become soggy. It is all right to put a hot filling into a hot crust, if you are in a hurry, and then let them cool together. To be on the safe side, I always cool the filling and the crust before combining them.

Cool filling + cool crust = crisp crust
Hot filling + hot crust = crisp crust
Hot filling + cool crust = soggy crust
Cool filling + hot crust = soggy crust

PIE PANS

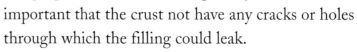

GLASS PIE PANS hold heat well and therefore help to brown the bottom of the crust. They also allow you to see the bottom of the pie while it is baking and to check for doneness. Although metal pie pans do not hold heat as well or distribute it as evenly, you will achieve better results with a dark metal pan than with one that is shiny. You may also want to punch a few holes in metal pie pans to help the crust bake better and crispier. (Metal pie pans with holes punched in them by the manufacturer are sometimes available, particularly in antique shops.) If you are using a pan with holes, it is especially important that the crust not have any cracks or holes through which the filling could leak.

One last word concerning pie pan sizes: Unfortunately, pie pans of the same diameter do not always have the same capacity. They can vary by up to 1 cup in the amount of filling they hold. There are ten 9-inch pie pans in my baking drawer, each with a slightly different capacity. My favorite pan is a 9-inch Pyrex or Corningware pan with a 4-cup capacity; for a 10-inch pie, I use a Pyrex pan with a capacity of 6 cups.

To be on the safe side, measure the capacities of your pans by filling them with water, 1 cup at a time. If you have too much filling, you can either bake the excess in a separate small dish as a treat for yourself, or discard it. Assuming that the diameters of your pans are the same, use the one that holds the most. Disposable pie pans, in particular, tend to be shallow.

SWEET CHEESE
RASPBERRY PIE

I ONCE WON a cheesecake-baking contest with a recipe similar to this one. This pie is not New York style—it is creamier—and can be made with pitted sour cherries or any type of firm, sweet berry.

Crust

| 1¾ | cups graham cracker crumbs or 21 graham cracker squares |
| 7 | tablespoons unsalted butter, melted |

Filling

2	cups fresh or frozen raspberries, drained if necessary
1	pound cream cheese, softened at room temperature
½	cup sugar
¼	teaspoon salt
2	large eggs plus 1 large egg yolk
1	teaspoon lemon juice, freshly squeezed

Topping

1	cup sour cream
2	tablespoons sugar
1	teaspoon vanilla

Raspberry Glaze

2	tablespoons sugar
1	tablespoon cornstarch
1	tablespoon lemon juice, freshly squeezed
2	cups fresh or frozen, drained raspberries

SWEET CHEESE RASPBERRY PIE

ART:

Cindy Kane

New York, New York

Mixed media

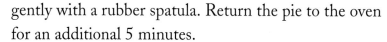

CRUST PREPARATION

If you are using graham cracker squares, crush them into fine crumbs in a food processor or put them into a plastic bag and crush them with a rolling pin. Put the crumbs and butter into a 10-inch pie pan and use your fingers to mix them together. Press the crumbs onto the bottom and sides of the pie pan.

FILLING PREPARATION

Preheat the oven to 375 degrees F.

Spread the raspberries over the bottom of the crust and refrigerate.

Beat the cream cheese, sugar and salt until absolutely smooth. Beat in the eggs, egg yolk and lemon juice. Pour the batter over the berries.

BAKING AND TOPPING PREPARATION

Bake the pie for 25 minutes.

While the pie is baking, stir together the sour cream, sugar and vanilla.

Remove the pie from the oven. Increase the oven temperature to 450 degrees. Spoon the sour-cream mixture over the top of the pie as evenly as possible and smooth

gently with a rubber spatula. Return the pie to the oven for an additional 5 minutes.

Cool the pie at room temperature for about 30 minutes and refrigerate it until completely cold, at least 2 hours. Once cold, the pie should be loosely wrapped with plastic until it is served.

GLAZE PREPARATION

If possible, prepare the raspberry glaze about 1 hour before serving the pie. It is best at room temperature. If you must make it further ahead, refrigerate it.

In a small saucepan, stir together sugar, cornstarch and lemon juice. Gently stir in 1 cup of the berries. Place the pan over medium heat and bring the glaze to a simmer, stirring constantly, until it is thick and translucent. Remove it from the heat. (Add 1 to 2 tablespoons water if it is too thick.) Press the mixture through a sieve. Gently stir in the remaining 1 cup berries.

Just before serving, top the pie with the raspberry glaze.

MAKES ONE 10-INCH SINGLE-CRUST PIE.

Susan's Unbaked
Blueberry Pie

THE BLUEBERRY FILLING—berries that are lightly sweetened and thickened—cooks quickly and is done on the stovetop so the kitchen remains cool. Lemon sherbet is an excellent topping for this summer pie.

1	prebaked 10-inch cornmeal pie shell (page 10)
7	cups fresh blueberries, washed, well drained, stems removed
1¼	cups sugar
¼	cup cornstarch
3	tablespoons lemon juice, freshly squeezed

Susan's Unbaked Blueberry Pie

ART:

Cameron Sweeting
Arlington, Virginia

Rue Capri
Washington, D.C.

Gesso, sand, acrylic, ribbon & Mylar

Prepare the pie shell.

Arrange half the blueberries in the baked pie shell.

In a large nonaluminum saucepan, stir together the sugar and cornstarch. Stir in the lemon juice and the remaining blueberries. Bring the berries to a simmer over medium heat. Cook them until they pop and the juices thicken slightly, about 5 to 6 minutes. Pour the cooked berries over the raw berries in the shell, spreading them as evenly as possible.

Refrigerate the pie for at least 2 hours before serving.

MAKES ONE 10-INCH SINGLE-CRUST PIE.

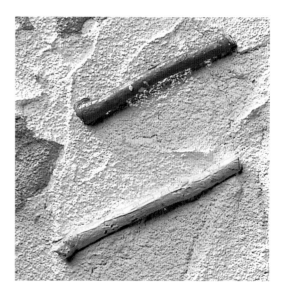

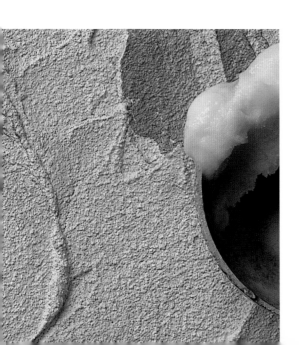

V. MONTENEGRO 90

Figgy Almond Pie

Figgy Almond Pie

ART:

Valerie Montenegro

Washington, D.C.

Colored pencil

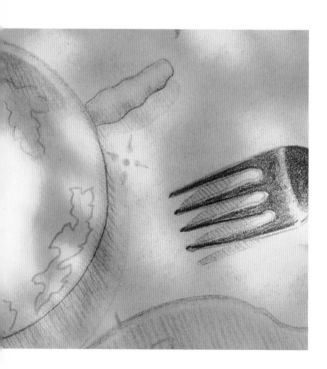

FIG PIE ORIGINATED as another means to stuff myself on these sensual fruits when they are ripe and available, which is not often enough. As it turned out, however, the pie was a much greater success when made with the more readily accessible dried figs: the delicacy of fresh figs is not concentrated enough to stand up to a batter or to baking. This is more of a teatime pie than a dinnertime finale. Moist and cakey, the pie combines the faint bitterness of almonds with the figs' sweet crunch.

Note: Either sweetened crème fraîche or sour cream is a delicious accompaniment to this pie. (Crème fraîche, cultured heavy cream, is available in gourmet grocery stores.) Stir 2 tablespoons sugar into 1 cup crème fraîche or sour cream. Set the cream aside for 20 minutes to allow the sugar to dissolve.

1	recipe basic pie crust for one 9-inch single-crust pie (page 9)
8	ounces (about 12) dried figs
6	tablespoons amaretto liqueur
½	cup almonds, blanched or unblanched
2	tablespoons all-purpose flour
½	cup unsalted butter, softened
½	cup light brown sugar, firmly packed
¼	teaspoon salt
2	large eggs
1	teaspoon grated lemon zest

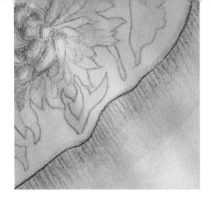

Roll out the pie dough and use it to line a 9-inch pie pan. Trim and crimp the edge. Refrigerate the pie shell while you make the filling.

Preheat the oven to 350 degrees F.

Use scissors or a small knife to remove the tough stems from the figs and cut each fig into quarters. Stir the figs and amaretto together in a small saucepan. Bring them to a boil over high heat. Remove the pan from the heat and cover it.

Grind the almonds and flour together in a blender or food processor until very fine.

In a medium mixing bowl, cream the butter, brown sugar and salt together until smooth. Beat in the eggs, one at a time. Drain the figs and pour their liquid into the butter and sugar mixture. Stir in the lemon zest and then the ground almond mixture.

Arrange the figs in the pie shell and spoon the filling over them. Spread it smooth with a rubber spatula. Bake the pie 35 to 40 minutes, until it is firm and nicely browned on top. Serve warm or cool with a dollop of sweetened crème fraîche or sour cream, if desired.

Tip: To make grating lemon zest easier, press a piece of wax paper down on a finely perforated grater. Rub the lemon over the paper-covered grater. (The paper will not tear.) Carefully remove the paper and scrape off the zest.

MAKES ONE 9-INCH SINGLE-CRUST PIE.

BETTY LOU'S RHUBARB PIE

Betty Lou Skutley of northern Wisconsin liked to make this pie for her family. The filling is not all fruit; instead, it is sturdier, the rhubarb fortified with eggs and a little flour. It is best made with a butter crust, especially when the top crust is rolled very thin.

For information on buying and freezing rhubarb, see page 134.

1	recipe basic pie dough for one 9-inch double-crust pie (page 9)

Filling

2	large eggs
1½	cups sugar
3	tablespoons all-purpose flour
1	teaspoon ground cinnamon
¼	teaspoon ground nutmeg
⅛	teaspoon salt
3½	cups diced (½-inch pieces) fresh raw rhubarb or frozen, slightly thawed
2	tablespoons unsalted butter, cut into thin slices

Egg Wash

1	large egg yolk, beaten with 1 tablespoon milk

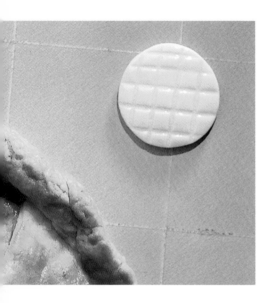

BETTY LOU'S RHUBARB PIE

ART:

Limor Dekel

Silver Spring, Maryland

Mixed media

CRUST PREPARATION

Roll out the larger piece of the pie dough and use it to line a 9-inch pie pan. Trim the edge but do not crimp it. Refrigerate the pie shell while you make the filling.

FILLING PREPARATION

Preheat the oven to 400 degrees F.

In a large bowl, beat the eggs well. Beat in the sugar, flour, cinnamon, nutmeg and salt. With a wooden spoon, gently stir in the diced rhubarb.

ASSEMBLY AND BAKING

Spoon the filling into the pie shell and dot the top of the filling with the butter slices.

Roll out the smaller piece of the dough as thin as possible and cut it into long strips about 1½ inches wide. Use the strips to create a lattice top on the pie, trimming the strips as needed. Fold the ends of the strips into the edge of the pie shell, pressing to seal them tightly.

Brush the lattice and crust edge with the egg wash.

Bake for 10 minutes, then reduce the oven temperature to 350 degrees and bake for about 1 hour more, until the top is very brown and shiny. Let the pie cool on a rack for at least 30 minutes before serving.

MAKES ONE 9-INCH DOUBLE-CRUST PIE.

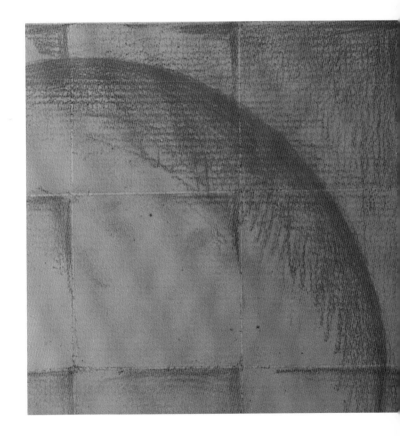

Maple Sugar
and Cream Pie

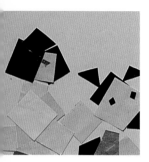

MOST OF THE INGREDIENTS for this pie can be found in the pantry. The pie looks very plain and doesn't take long to make but tastes wonderful. A spoonful of cider vinegar is the "mystery ingredient."

Note: If maple sugar is unavailable, reduce the heavy cream by 2 tablespoons and replace the maple sugar with ½ cup maple syrup.

1   **prebaked 9-inch pie shell (page 9)**

Filling

½   **cup maple sugar**
½   **cup light brown sugar, firmly packed**
¼   **cup all-purpose flour**
¼   **teaspoon salt**
1   **tablespoon cider vinegar**
1½   **cups heavy cream**

Topping

2   **teaspoons sugar**
1   **teaspoon ground cinnamon**
2   **tablespoons unsalted butter, cut into small pieces**

Whipped cream and additional cinnamon and sugar for garnishing (optional)

Maple Sugar and Cream Pie

ART:

Claire Cole

Bethesda, Maryland

Magazaic

FILLING PREPARATION

Preheat the oven to 400 degrees F.

In a medium mixing bowl, stir together the maple sugar, brown sugar, flour and salt. Stir in the cider vinegar and whisk in the heavy cream.

TOPPING PREPARATION

In a small bowl, stir together the sugar and the cinnamon.

ASSEMBLY AND BAKING

Put the pie pan on a sheet pan. Pour the filling into the prebaked pie shell. Drop small pieces of butter over the top of the pie and sprinkle the surface with the cinnamon sugar.

Bake for 45 minutes. The center of the pie will still be a little jiggly, but it will firm up as the pie cools. Cool on a rack for 1 hour at room temperature before serving. You also may refrigerate this pie and serve it cold.

To decorate, add a spoonful of unsweetened whipped cream and an additional sprinkling of cinnamon sugar to each slice, if desired.

MAKES ONE 9-INCH SINGLE-CRUST PIE.

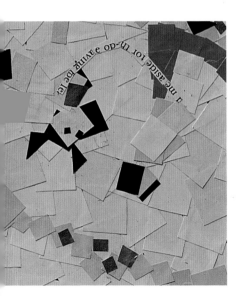

Cranberry-Pear Streusel Pie

Cranberry-Pear Streusel Pie

HOMEY AND CASUAL, this pie starts with my family's traditional cranberry sauce, which calls for a whole chopped orange and brandy. Cranberries have such a sparkly sour bite that they accent the sweetness of ripe pears perfectly.

Buy lots of fresh cranberries just before Thanksgiving when there are plenty at the grocery store. Double-bagged, they will stay fresh in the freezer.

Streusel Crust

2	**cups rolled oats (not quick-cooking)**
⅔	**cup light brown sugar, firmly packed**
¼	**teaspoon ground cloves**
10	**tablespoons (1¼ sticks) unsalted butter, cut into pieces**

Filling

½	**medium seedless orange, coarsely chopped**
1	**cup sugar**
¼	**cup water**
2	**cups (8 ounces) cranberries, washed, stems removed**
¼	**cup brandy (optional)**
4	**medium, firm, ripe Bosc, Bartlett or Anjou pears**

ART:

Nina Strucko
Westminster, Maryland
Watercolor

38

STREUSEL CRUST PREPARATION

In a medium mixing bowl, stir together the rolled oats, brown sugar and cloves. Rub the butter pieces into the dry ingredients until the mixture is crumbly and still somewhat lumpy. Set the streusel aside while you prepare the filling.

FILLING PREPARATION

Pulverize the orange half (peel and all) in a food processor or blender.

Put the sugar and water in a medium nonaluminum saucepan. Bring the mixture to a boil over medium heat and let it continue to boil for 3 minutes. Add the cranberries and chopped orange and boil until all the berries pop. Let the berries cool for 15 minutes and stir in the brandy, if using. Peel and core the pears, cut them into 1-inch chunks and put them into a large mixing bowl. Stir the cranberries into the pears.

ASSEMBLY AND BAKING

Preheat the oven to 350 degrees F.

Press two-thirds (about 2¼ cups) of the streusel mixture onto the bottom and sides of a 10-inch pie pan. Spoon the fruit into the pie pan. Sprinkle the remaining streusel over top of the fruit. Set the pie pan on a baking sheet.

Bake for 50 to 55 minutes, until browned and very bubbly. _____

MAKES ONE 10-INCH DOUBLE-CRUST PIE.

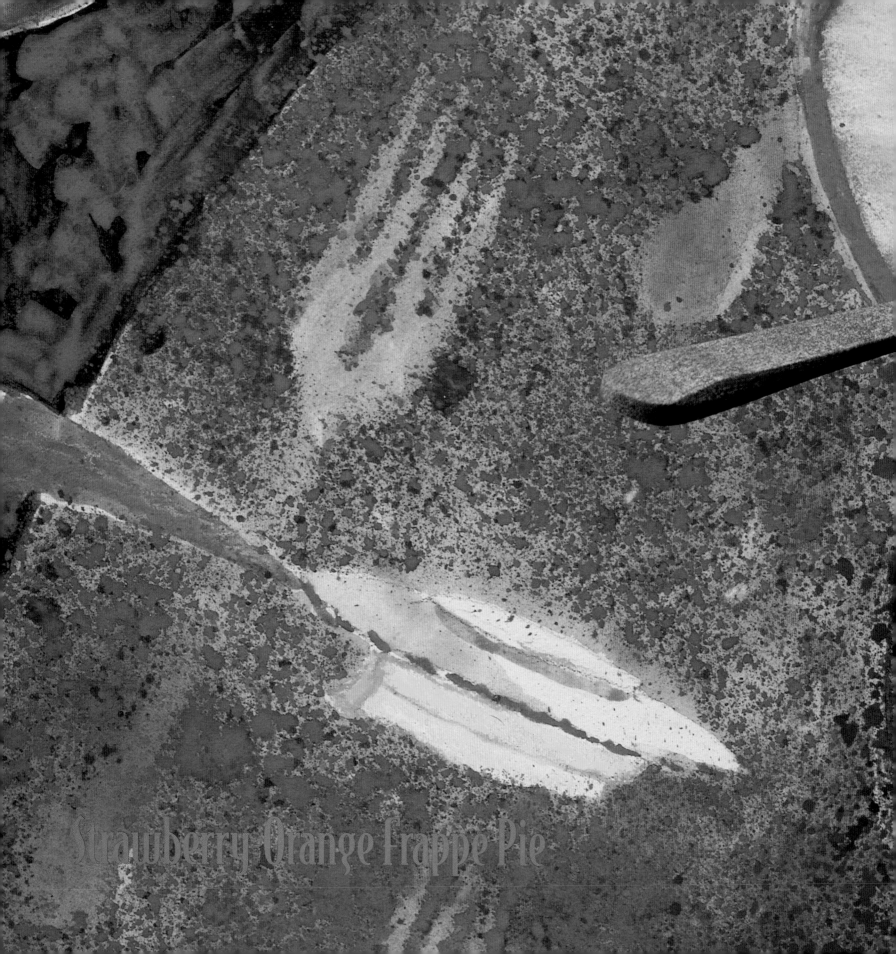

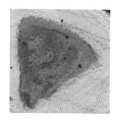

Strawberry-Orange Frappe Pie

ART:

Frances Connelly

Kansas City, Missouri

Watercolor, gouache & pastel

KIDS AND ADULTS ALIKE love this chilly ice cream pie, which is dotted with bits of fresh strawberry and accented with orange juice and candied peel.

Let your strawberries ripen as much as possible to deepen their flavor. A few soft spots are okay; trim them with a small knife before chopping the berries.

3   **medium juice oranges**

Crust

1¾   **cups graham cracker crumbs or 21 graham cracker squares**

7   **tablespoons unsalted butter, melted**

Filling

1   **pint good-quality vanilla ice cream**

1   **generous pint (1 pound) very ripe strawberries, finely chopped, plus a few additional for garnishing**

½   **cup sugar**

½   **teaspoon orange extract**

1   **package unflavored gelatin**

Candied Orange Peel

1   **cup sugar**

¼   **cup water**

42

ORANGE PREPARATION

Grate the zest from 1 of the oranges and set it aside. With a carrot peeler, remove the peel from the other 2 oranges and set aside. Squeeze 1 (or 2, if necessary) of the oranges until you have ½ cup of orange juice and set it aside. Refrigerate any unsqueezed oranges for another use.

CRUST PREPARATION

Preheat the oven to 400 degrees F.

If you are using graham cracker squares, crush them into fine crumbs in a food processor or put them into a plastic bag and crush them with a rolling pin. Put the crumbs, butter and reserved grated orange zest into a 10-inch pie pan and use your fingers to mix them together. Press the crumb mixture onto the bottom and sides of the pie pan. Bake for 6 minutes and then set the pie crust in the refrigerator to chill.

FILLING PREPARATION

Set the ice cream in the refrigerator to soften. Toss the chopped strawberries with the sugar and orange extract.

Put the reserved orange juice in a small heatproof bowl and sprinkle the gelatin over it. Put 1 inch of water in a small saucepan and set the bowl of gelatin in the water. Place the saucepan over low heat and let the gelatin melt, stirring until it dissolves.

Meanwhile, put the ice cream in a mixing bowl and beat it on low speed to soften it further. Add the strawberries to the ice cream and blend until they are evenly distributed. When the gelatin is completely smooth, whisk it slowly into the ice cream. Beat the mixture another 30 seconds or so. Scrape down the sides of the bowl and put it into the freezer for 10 minutes. After the pie filling has cooled and firmed slightly, beat it again on high speed for 2 minutes. Pour the filling into the graham cracker crust, cover with plastic wrap and freeze until firm, about 2 hours.

CANDIED ORANGE PEEL PREPARATION

Cut the reserved orange peel into thin slivers with a sharp knife. Put the peel into a small saucepan with the sugar and water. Bring the mixture to a boil and let it continue to boil for 2 to 3 minutes, or until large bubbles form on the surface. While it is cooking, oil a sheet pan lightly with vegetable oil. Remove the peels with a fork and lay the strips on the sheet pan to cool and harden.

To serve, set the pie in the refrigerator for 10 minutes before cutting it. Decorate each slice with a few strawberries and some candied orange peel.

MAKES ONE 10-INCH SINGLE-CRUST PIE.

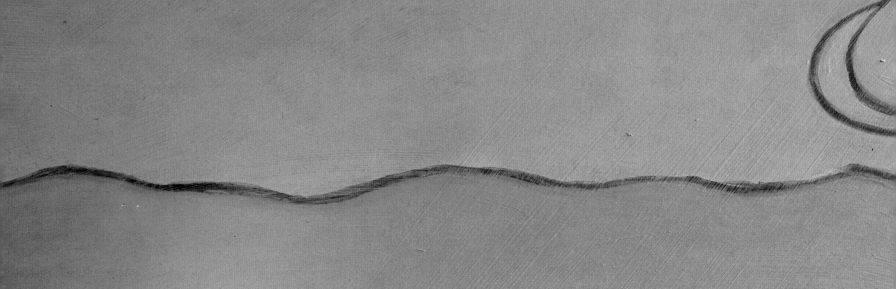

Lemon-Lime Slice Pie

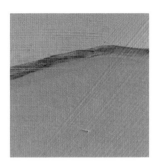

Lemon-Lime Slice Pie

ART:

Craig Cahoon

Washington, D.C.

Acrylic

EARLY 19TH-CENTURY Shakers created the recipe for lemon-slice pie. Necessary to a healthy diet, citrus was particularly precious to the northern Shakers, as it was something they could not grow themselves. Using the whole unpeeled lemon wasted none of the fruit. This rendition, adapted to accommodate modern thick-skinned lemons and limes, is not for the faint of heart. The peels are no longer baked inside the pie as they once were, but this is still a double-citrus whammy.

1	recipe basic pie dough for one 9-inch double-crust pie (page 9)
4	medium lemons
2	medium limes
2	cups water
1¾	cups sugar
1	teaspoon salt
4	large eggs plus 1 large egg, separated
2	tablespoons sugar for sprinkling on top of the pie

Roll out the larger piece of the pie dough and use it to line a 9-inch pie pan. Trim the edge and refrigerate the pie shell while you prepare the filling.

Preheat the oven to 450 degrees F.

Use a vegetable peeler to remove the zest from 1 of the lemons and 1 of the limes. With a sharp knife, slice the zest into very thin slivers. In a small pot, bring the water to a boil. Blanch the zest in the water for 1 to 2 minutes. Drain the zest and put it in a medium mixing bowl.

Using a small, sharp knife, remove and discard the pith from the first lime and lemon, then the peel and pith from the remaining lime and the remaining 3 lemons. Remove the segments from the fruit by slicing next to the membranes with the knife. Add the fruit to the blanched zest. Stir in the sugar and salt. In a separate bowl, beat the 4 eggs and 1 egg yolk together and stir them into the limes and lemons.

Spoon the filling into the pie shell. Roll out the smaller piece of the dough and cover the pie with it. Trim and crimp the edge.

Beat the remaining egg white. Brush the top of the pie with the beaten white and sprinkle the pie with the 2 tablespoons sugar. Cut slits in the top of the crust to allow the steam to escape while the pie bakes.

Bake for 10 minutes, then reduce the heat to 350 degrees and bake 40 to 45 more minutes, until firm to the touch and well browned. Let the pie cool on a rack for at least 1 hour before serving.

MAKES ONE 9-INCH DOUBLE-CRUST PIE.

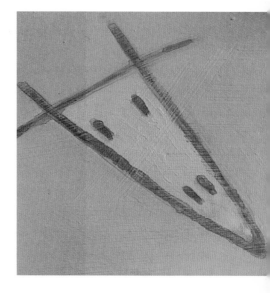

Backyard Green Tomato Pie

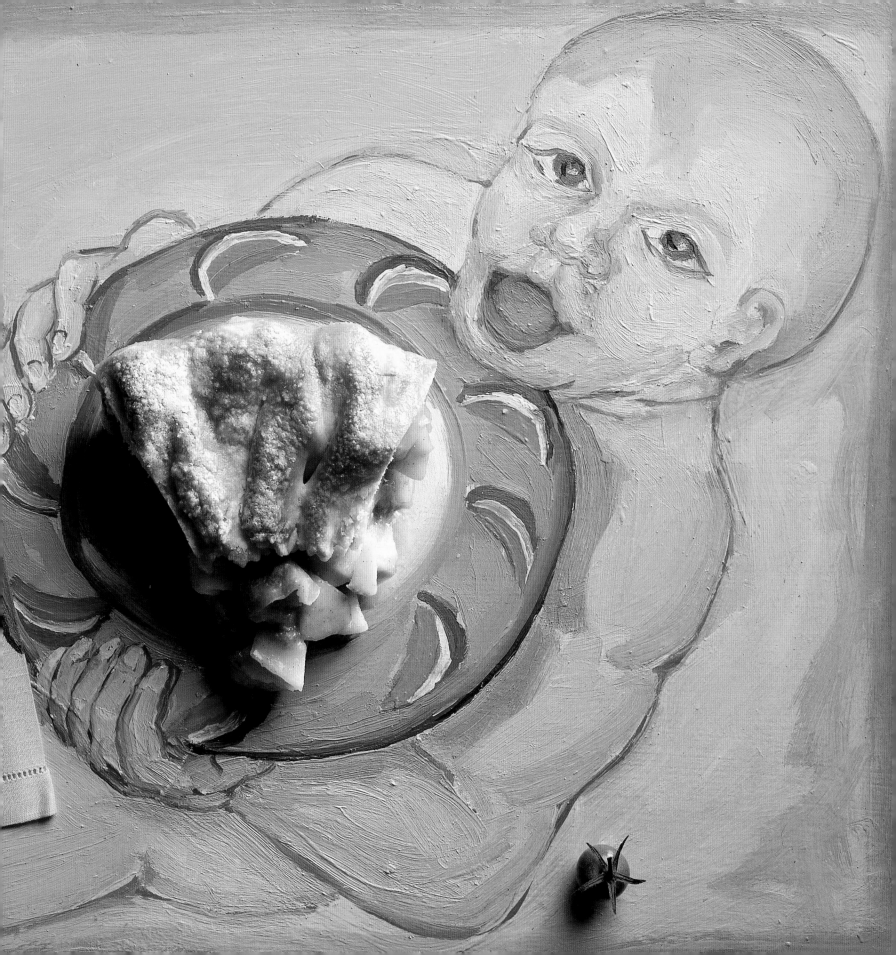

Backyard Green Tomato Pie

GREEN TOMATO PIE originated, I'm sure, for the same reason that I first made it. One day in late fall, I was visiting friends who had an ample backyard boasting a gnarled apple tree and several bountiful tomato vines. The tree was loaded with small, ugly apples, and the tomato vines drooped with unripened fruit. We made both plain apple pie and green tomato pie that day. In spite of much skepticism, the green tomato pie disappeared before the plain apple pie. This is an excellent way to use the last of the tomato harvest.

Note: This pie also can be baked as a standard double-crust pie. Follow the crust directions for Apricot and White Cherry Pie (page 78).

ART:

Tom Osgood

Takoma Park, Maryland

Oil

50

1	recipe basic pie dough for one 10-inch double-crust pie (page 9)

Filling

6	medium, very tart, firm apples, such as Winesap or Granny Smith, peeled, cored and cut into chunks
4	medium or 6 small green tomatoes, unpeeled, cored and cut into 1-inch chunks (do not use sauce tomatoes)
2	tablespoons currants (optional)
¾	cup sugar
6	tablespoons all-purpose flour
¼	cup light brown sugar, firmly packed
2	teaspoons quick-cooking tapioca
1	teaspoon ground cinnamon
½	teaspoon ground ginger
¼	teaspoon salt
3	tablespoons unsalted butter, cut into small pieces

Egg Wash and Topping

1	large egg, beaten with 1 tablespoon milk
1	tablespoon sugar

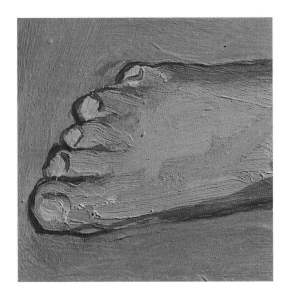

FILLING PREPARATION

First, prepare the pie dough.

Preheat the oven to 400 degrees F.

In a large mixing bowl, stir together the apples, tomatoes and currants, if using. In a small mixing bowl, stir together the sugar, flour, brown sugar, tapioca, cinnamon, ginger and salt. Sprinkle the sugar mixture over the fruit and toss everything together thoroughly. Set the filling aside while you roll out the crust.

ASSEMBLY AND BAKING

Without dividing the dough, roll it out into a very large circle, approximately 20 inches in diameter. Use a pastry wheel or small, sharp knife to trim the dough to a circle 18 inches in diameter. Fit the dough into the pie pan, letting it extend over the sides and onto the countertop. Spoon the filling into the pie shell. Dot the top of the fruit with the butter pieces. Lift the edges of the crust and bring them in over the filling. The folds will be

uneven and the crust will not completely cover the filling. There should be a hole in the center.

Brush the pie crust lightly with the egg wash. Sprinkle the entire pie with 1 tablespoon sugar.

Put the pie on a sheet pan and bake it for 20 minutes. Reduce the temperature to 350 degrees and bake an additional 40 minutes or so, until the crust is a beautiful brown and the filling is bubbling. Let cool on a rack 1 hour before serving.

MAKES ONE 10-INCH DOUBLE-CRUST PIE.

51

Fresh Peach Pie

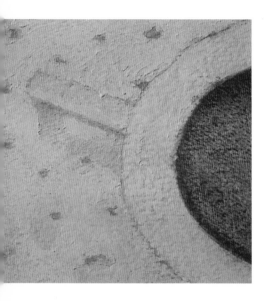

Fresh Peach Pie

ART:

Micki Kirk

Washington, D.C.

Oil pastel & Prismacolor

NUTMEG IS JUST THE RIGHT spice for this simple pie. While it is still warm, it is difficult to cut, but it tastes great anyway—well worth the aesthetic sacrifice. It's even better served with peach ice cream.

I like the effect of the full amount of nutmeg, but it can be decreased to ½ teaspoon, or to taste.

1	prebaked 9-inch pie shell (page 9)
¾	cup plus ¼ cup water
1	cup sugar
1	tablespoon lemon juice, freshly squeezed
¼	cup cornstarch
1	teaspoon ground nutmeg
7	fresh, ripe, medium peaches

Prepare the pie shell.

In a large nonaluminum saucepan, stir together the ¾ cup water, sugar and lemon juice. Over medium heat, bring the sugar mixture to a boil; remove from the heat.

Dissolve the cornstarch completely in the remaining ¼ cup water and stir it into the hot liquid. Add the nutmeg. Over low heat, while stirring constantly, continue to cook the liquid until thickened and clear. Set aside to cool.

Bring a large pot of water to a boil. Immerse the peaches for 30 seconds and remove them with a slotted spoon. Let them cool for a minute or two and remove the skins with a small, sharp knife. Pit and cut the peaches into ½-inch slices. Stir them into the cornstarch mixture and spoon the filling into the prebaked pie shell.

Serve the pie either warm (when it will be a little messy) or after it has cooled completely in the refrigerator.

MAKES ONE 9-INCH SINGLE-CRUST PIE.

Cool Lime Pie With Tequila

REFRESHINGLY TART on a hot summer's day, this is similar to a Key lime pie, with the added punch of tequila. It needs no gelatin and has a lovely texture. Serve with or without the whipped cream.

Cool Lime Pie With Tequila

Crust

1½	cups graham cracker crumbs or 18 graham cracker squares
6	tablespoons unsalted butter, melted

Filling

1	can (14 ounces) sweetened condensed milk
1	tablespoon grated lime zest
½	cup lime juice, freshly squeezed (from 3 medium or 2 large limes)
3	tablespoons tequila
¼	teaspoon salt
1	cup heavy cream for topping (optional) Sliced limes for garnishing

ART:

Janice Olson

Washington, D.C.

Watercolor & acrylic

CRUST PREPARATION

Preheat the oven to 350 degrees F.

If you are using graham cracker squares, crush them into fine crumbs in a food processor or put them into a plastic bag and crush them with a rolling pin. Put the crumbs and butter into a 9-inch pie pan and use your fingers to mix them together. Press the crumb mixture onto the bottom and sides of the pan. Bake for 8 minutes and set the pie crust aside to cool.

FILLING PREPARATION

In a medium mixing bowl, beat together the condensed milk, lime zest, lime juice, tequila and salt. Set the filling aside for about 5 minutes, until slightly thickened. Pour the filling into the crust and refrigerate for at least 2 hours.

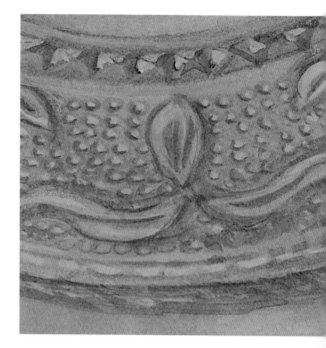

Just before serving, beat the heavy cream until stiff peaks form and cover the top of the pie with it, if desired. Serve the pie cold, garnished with lime slices.

Tip: To make grating lime zest easier, press a piece of wax paper down on a finely perforated grater. Rub the lime over the paper-covered grater. (The paper will not tear.) Carefully remove the paper and scrape off the zest.

MAKES ONE 9-INCH SINGLE-CRUST PIE.

Apple Butter Apple Pie

SOME 18TH- AND 19TH-CENTURY pie recipes required the apples to be poached and then pureed into a concoction resembling apple butter. In this modern version, apple butter enriches the fresh apple filling and thickens the juices slightly. A dash of chili powder adds spice. A little lard in the crust gives an especially flaky shell.

Apple butter is found next to the jams and jellies in the grocery store.

Apple Butter Apple Pie

1	**recipe basic pie dough for one 10-inch double-crust pie (page 9)**

Filling

2–2½	**pounds (about 8–9 medium) Granny Smith, Pippin or other firm, tart apples that will hold their shape when baked (7 cups sliced)**
⅓	**cup apple butter**
2	**tablespoons lemon juice, freshly squeezed**
¾	**cup sugar**
6	**tablespoons all-purpose flour**
½	**teaspoon ground cinnamon**
¼	**teaspoon ground cloves**
⅛	**teaspoon chili powder**
2	**tablespoons unsalted butter, cut into small pieces**

Egg Wash

1	**large egg yolk, beaten with 2 tablespoons milk**

ART:

Mary Sherman

Boston, Massachusetts

Mixed media

Reduce the oven temperature to 350 degrees and let the pie continue to bake until it has browned nicely and the fruit is bubbling out around the edges, 30 to 35 minutes.

Let cool on a rack at least 30 minutes before serving.

MAKES ONE 10-INCH DOUBLE-CRUST PIE.

CRUST PREPARATION

Roll out the larger piece of the pie dough and use it to line a 10-inch pie pan. Trim the edge and refrigerate the pie shell while you prepare the filling.

FILLING PREPARATION

Preheat the oven to 400 degrees F.

Peel and core the apples and slice them into ¼-inch slices. Put the apple slices into a large mixing bowl. Stir the apple butter and lemon juice into the apple slices.

In a separate mixing bowl, stir together the sugar, flour, cinnamon, cloves and chili powder. Sprinkle the dry ingredients over the apples and stir thoroughly with a wooden spoon.

ASSEMBLY AND BAKING

Spoon the fruit into the pie shell. Dot the top of the filling with the butter pieces.

Roll out the smaller piece of the dough and cover the pie with it. Trim and crimp the edge. Brush the top of the pie with the egg wash. Cut a few slits in the crust with a sharp knife to allow the steam to escape while the pie is baking.

Set the pie on a sheet pan and bake for 30 minutes.

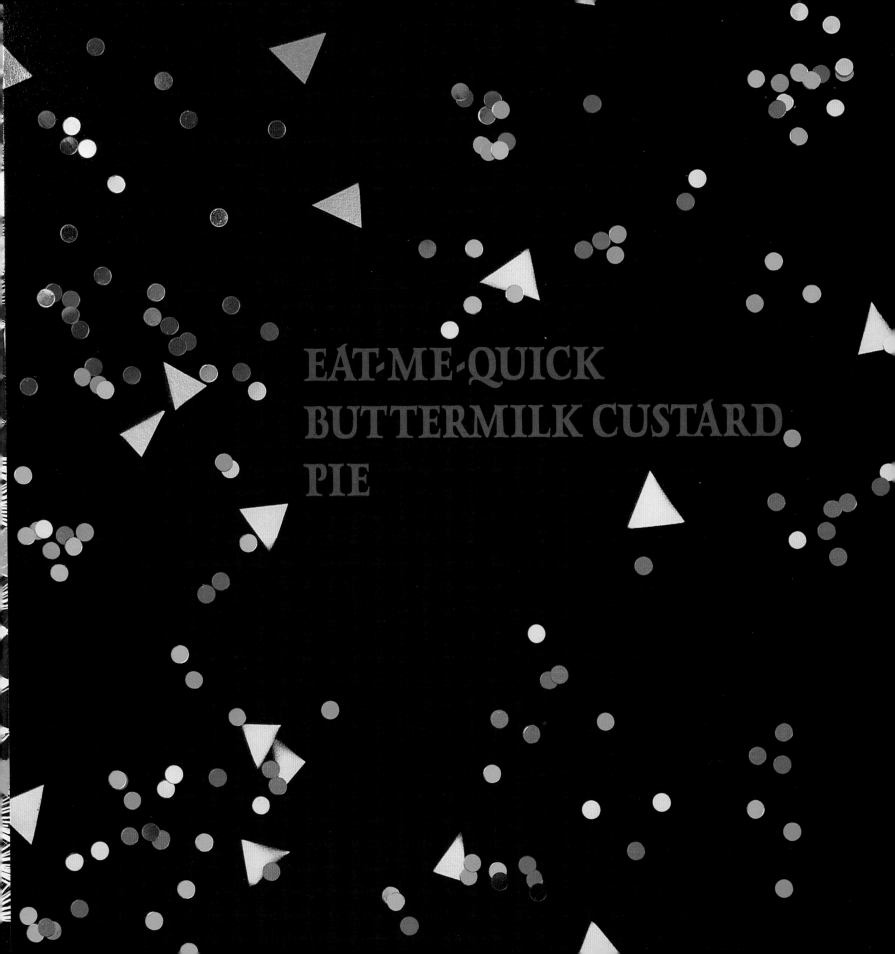

EAT·ME·QUICK
BUTTERMILK CUSTARD
PIE

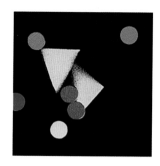

EAT·ME·QUICK BUTTERMILK CUSTARD PIE

BECAUSE BUTTERMILK is low in fat, it makes a tender custard. Sliced fruit or fresh cold berries make a good topping for this pie, whose taste is reminiscent of light cheesecake, with a delicate lemon flavor.

ART:

Stephanie Shieldhouse

Jacksonville, Florida

Scratchboard & foil

1	prebaked 9-inch pie shell (page 9)
2	tablespoons unsalted butter
¾	cup sugar
2	large eggs, separated, plus 2 large egg yolks
2	tablespoons lemon juice, freshly squeezed
¼	cup all-purpose flour
¼	teaspoon salt
2½	cups buttermilk

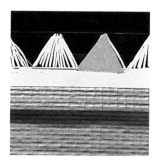

Prepare the pie shell.

Preheat the oven to 425 degrees F.

Cream the butter and sugar together. Add the 4 egg yolks, 1 at a time, beating the mixture after each addition until it becomes light and fluffy. Stir in the lemon juice, flour and salt. Whisk in the buttermilk.

In a separate bowl, beat the 2 egg whites until they hold soft peaks. Stir the whites into the custard with a whisk.

Set the prebaked pie shell on a sheet pan and pour the custard into it. Bake for 15 minutes. Reduce the oven temperature to 350 degrees and bake for 30 to 35 minutes more, or until a knife inserted in the center of the pie comes out clean. Cool on a rack at room temperature for 15 minutes and then in the refrigerator for at least 1 hour.

_____

MAKES ONE 9-INCH SINGLE-CRUST PIE.

Mom's Lemon Meringue Pie

As my mother tells it, at 14 she was a 4-H Club member and wanted to enter a lemon meringue pie at the county fair. Practicing, she baked many pies until she perfected this recipe, which took the blue ribbon. As luck would have it, she married a man who loved lemon meringue. Here is the recipe—the blue-ribbon winner and my father's favorite pie.

Mom's Lemon Meringue Pie

1	prebaked 9-inch pie shell (page 9)

Filling

¾	cup sugar
6	tablespoons cornstarch
½	teaspoon salt
1½	cups water
3	large egg yolks (reserve whites for meringue)
2	tablespoons unsalted butter
1½	tablespoons grated lemon zest
¼	cup lemon juice, freshly squeezed (from 1 large lemon)

Meringue

3	large egg whites, room temperature
¼	teaspoon cream of tartar
6	tablespoons sugar

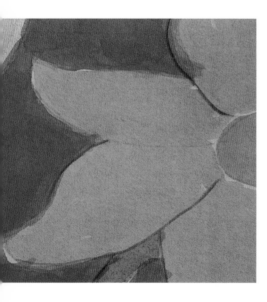

ART:

Rebecca Wood

Athens, Georgia

Watercolor

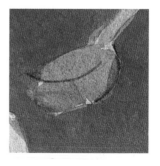

70

FILLING PREPARATION

First, prepare the pie shell.

Mix together the sugar, cornstarch and salt in a nonaluminum saucepan. Add the water a little at a time, stirring until smooth. Cook over low heat, stirring constantly, until the mixture boils and becomes thick, sticky and translucent.

Beat the egg yolks slightly. Add the hot sugar mixture a little at a time to the yolks, stirring quickly until the egg mixture is hot and smooth. Return the mixture to the saucepan, add the butter and cook over low heat, stirring constantly, until smooth and shiny, about 2 minutes.

Remove the pan from the burner and stir in the zest and lemon juice. Set the filling aside to cool for 30 minutes before spooning it into the prebaked pie shell. Smooth the filling with a small spatula or the back of a spoon.

MERINGUE PREPARATION

Preheat the oven to 350 degrees F.

Beat the egg whites with the cream of tartar until they hold soft peaks. Beat in the sugar, 1 tablespoon at a time, continuing to beat until very stiff but not dry.

Cover the filling with the meringue, creating peaks and swirls with the back of a spoon. Make sure that the meringue touches the edge of the pie shell all the way around.

Bake until the meringue is golden, about 12 to 15 minutes. Allow the pie to cool at room temperature for 1 hour and then refrigerate it until completely cold, at least 1 hour.

Tip: To make grating lemon zest easier, press a piece of wax paper down on a finely perforated grater. Rub the lemon over the paper-covered grater. (The paper will not tear.) Carefully remove the paper and scrape off the zest.

MAKES ONE 9-INCH SINGLE-CRUST PIE.

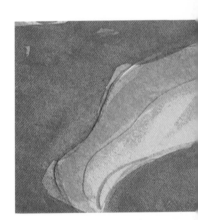

Ultrasmooth Chocolate Malted Pie

THERE IS NO IMPROVING the luscious texture of chocolate, heavy cream and lots of egg yolks. The better the chocolate, the better the pie. Do not use chocolate sold as "baking chocolate." Instead, check the candy aisle of the grocery store for premium chocolates, such as those made by Tobler or Lindt. A little unsweetened whipped cream makes a good topping.

Malt powder is another of the all-time great food inventions. A product of malted barley and wheat, it is too good to use in milk shakes only. It is found in supermarkets in the cocoa section.

Crust

24	**chocolate wafers (⅔ of a 9-ounce box)**
4	**tablespoons unsalted butter, melted**
¼	**teaspoon salt**

Filling

7	**large egg yolks**
8	**ounces semisweet chocolate**
2	**cups heavy cream**
¼	**cup malt powder**

Ultrasmooth Chocolate Malted Pie

ART:

Doris Keil-Shamieh

Jefferson, Maryland

Collograph print collage

74

CRUST PREPARATION

Preheat the oven to 350 degrees F.

Crush the wafers into fine crumbs in a food processor or put them into a plastic bag and crush them with a rolling pin. You should have 1½ cups. Put the crumbs, butter and salt into a 9-inch pie pan and use your fingers to mix them together. Press the crumbs onto the bottom and sides of the pie pan. Bake for 6 minutes and set the pie crust aside to cool.

FILLING PREPARATION

In a medium mixing bowl, beat the egg yolks well and set them aside.

Chop the chocolate into small pieces and set it aside. Scald the cream in a medium heavy-bottomed saucepan. When the cream begins to steam, stir in the chocolate until it has melted completely.

Very gradually, pour the chocolate mixture into the egg yolks, stirring continuously as you pour. Pour the filling mixture back into the saucepan and set it over low heat. Continue to cook the filling, stirring it constantly, until it is steaming and has thickened to a puddinglike consistency, about 5 to 10 minutes. Do not let the filling boil.

With the mixture off the heat, stir in the malt powder.

Let the filling cool for 10 minutes and pour it into the pie shell. Before serving, cool the pie completely in the refrigerator, at least 2 hours.

MAKES ONE 9-INCH SINGLE-CRUST PIE.

Apricot and
White Cherry Pie

WITH ITS DELECTABLE BALANCE of tart and sweet summer fruits, this pie epitomizes homemade pastry. White cherries are not actually white, but pale yellow with a pink blush. Their sweetness needs the acidity of the apricots to counteract it. Fresh or frozen Queen Anne or Bing cherries make a fine substitute if white cherries are unavailable.

Note: A cherry pitter is a handy gadget and not expensive, but if you do not have one, the pits can be removed with the rounded end of a wire hairpin (not a bobby pin).

| 1 | recipe Flaky Citrus Pastry (page 10) |

Filling

1	cup sugar
3	tablespoons all-purpose flour
½	teaspoon ground nutmeg
1½	teaspoons grated orange zest
2	pounds fresh, ripe apricots
3	cups fresh or frozen white cherries
2	tablespoons unsalted butter, cut into small pieces

Egg Wash

| 1 | large egg yolk, beaten with 1 tablespoon milk |

APRICOT AND WHITE CHERRY PIE

ART:

Jacqueline Shaffer

Washington, D.C.

Pastel

CRUST PREPARATION

Roll out the larger piece of the pie dough and use it to line a 10-inch pie pan. Trim the edge and refrigerate the pie shell while you prepare the filling.

FILLING PREPARATION

First, preheat the oven to 400 degrees F.

Stir together the sugar, flour, nutmeg and orange zest in a large mixing bowl. Cut the apricots in half, discard the pits and add the apricot halves to the bowl. Stem and pit the cherries and add them (with their juice) to the apricots. Stir the filling until the dry ingredients are evenly distributed.

ASSEMBLY AND BAKING

Spoon the fruit into the pie shell. Dot the top of the filling with the butter pieces.

Roll out the smaller piece of the dough and cover the pie with it. Trim and crimp the edge. Brush the top of the pie with the egg wash. Cut a few slits in the crust with a sharp knife to allow the steam to escape while the pie is baking.

Set the pie on a sheet pan and bake for 30 minutes.

Reduce the oven temperature to 350 degrees and let the pie continue to bake until nicely browned and bubbling around the edges, about 30 minutes.

Let cool on a rack at least 30 minutes before serving.

Tip: To make grating orange zest easier, press a piece of wax paper down on a finely perforated grater. Rub the orange over the paper-covered grater. (The paper will not tear.) Carefully remove the paper and scrape off the zest.

MAKES ONE 10-INCH DOUBLE-CRUST PIE.

Summer Berry Chiffon Pie

THE BAKING ELITE may consider chiffon pies outdated, but I love their old-fashioned fanciness. Cool and creamy, this pie could be made with blackberries or black raspberries. If you want to gild the lily, consider using a cocoa crust (page 10).

1 **prebaked 9-inch pie shell (page 9)**

Filling

1 **pint fresh strawberries, washed, well drained, hulled and quartered**
1 **pint fresh raspberries**
1 **cup sugar**
¼ **cup orange juice**
2 **tablespoons lemon juice, freshly squeezed**
2 **teaspoons unflavored gelatin**
1 **cup heavy cream**

Topping

1 **cup heavy cream**
 Additional berries or sprinkles for decorating the top

Summer Berry Chiffon Pie

ART :

Carolyn Stachowski

Sterling, Virginia

Tempera paint collage

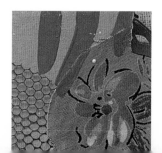

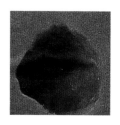

FILLING PREPARATION

First, prepare the pie shell.

Puree ½ cup strawberries and ½ cup raspberries together and strain the puree through a fine sieve into a bowl. Stir the remaining strawberries and raspberries into the puree. Stir in the sugar and set the mixture aside.

In a small heatproof bowl, stir together the orange juice and lemon juice. Sprinkle the gelatin over the juice and set it aside for 5 minutes to soften. Melt the gelatin by placing the bowl in a small saucepan of water set over low heat. Warm it, stirring, until it is smooth and clear. Stir the gelatin into the berry mixture and refrigerate the filling for about 20 minutes, until it begins to thicken slightly.

Beat the heavy cream until it holds stiff peaks. Fold the whipped cream into the berries and spoon the filling into the prebaked pie shell. Refrigerate for at least 2 hours, or up to 1 day, loosely wrapped in plastic.

TOPPING PREPARATION

Just before serving, beat the cream until stiff peaks form, and cover the pie with it. Decorate the top with strawberries, raspberries or sprinkles.

MAKES ONE 9-INCH SINGLE-CRUST PIE.

Very Berry Pie

OVERFLOWING WITH FRUIT, this pie is very juicy and fun to eat in a bowl with vanilla ice cream. It lends itself to various combinations of berries, depending on what is available. Start with blueberries and add 2 cups of any other combination.

Very Berry Pie

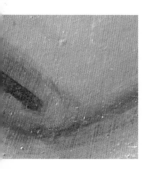

ART:

John Sapp

Rockville, Maryland

Acrylic

1	recipe basic pie dough for one 9-inch double-crust pie (page 9)
½	cup sugar or more to taste, up to 1 cup
¼	cup all-purpose flour
¼	teaspoon ground nutmeg
¼	teaspoon salt
1	tablespoon lemon juice, freshly squeezed
4	cups fresh blueberries, washed, stems removed, well drained, or frozen (not thawed)
2	cups raspberries, blackberries or boysenberries
1	tablespoon unsalted butter, cut into small pieces
½	tablespoon sugar for sprinkling over pie

Roll out the larger piece of the dough and use it to line a 9-inch pie pan. Trim the edge and refrigerate the pie shell while you prepare the filling.

Preheat the oven to 375 degrees F.

In a large mixing bowl, stir together the ½ cup sugar, flour, nutmeg, salt and lemon juice. Stir in the berries gently. Taste and add more sugar if necessary. Spoon the berry mixture into the pie shell.

Dot the top of the pie with the butter pieces.

Roll out the smaller piece of the dough and lay it over the top of the pie.

Trim and crimp the edge. Cut a few slits in the crust with a sharp knife to allow the steam to escape while the pie is baking. Sprinkle the top with sugar.

Set the pie on a sheet pan and bake until well browned and bubbling, about 50 to 55 minutes.

Let cool on a rack for at least 1 hour before serving.

———————

MAKES ONE 9-INCH DOUBLE-CRUST PIE.

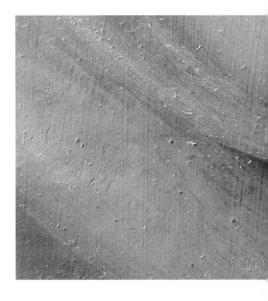

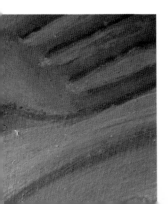

BRANDIED BUTTERSCOTCH PIE

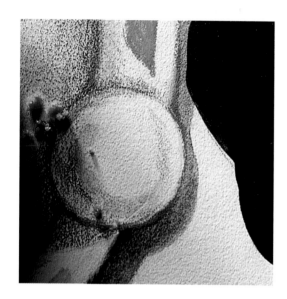

THIS RECIPE is a little less sweet and a little easier to prepare if you replace the meringue with freshly whipped, unsweetened cream. When it comes to gingersnaps for the crust, the spicier the better.

Crust

24	gingersnaps
4	tablespoons unsalted butter, melted

Filling

3	tablespoons cornstarch
3	cups half-and-half
6	large egg yolks (reserve whites for meringue)
¾	cup sugar
½	cup brandy
4	tablespoons unsalted butter

Meringue

6	egg whites, room temperature
6	tablespoons sugar

BRANDIED BUTTERSCOTCH PIE

ART:

Margaret Finch

Washington, D.C.

Acrylic & colored pencil

CRUST PREPARATION

Preheat the oven to 400 degrees F.

Crush the gingersnaps into crumbs in a food processor or put them into a plastic bag and crush them with a rolling pin. Put the crumbs and butter into a 10-inch pie pan and use your fingers to mix them together. Press the crumb mixture onto the bottom and sides of the pie pan. Bake for 6 minutes and then set the pie crust aside to cool.

FILLING PREPARATION

In a small bowl, stir together the cornstarch and ¼ cup half-and-half. In a medium bowl, beat the egg yolks lightly.

In a large heavy-bottomed saucepan, stir together the sugar and brandy. Set the saucepan over medium-high heat. Let the sugar come to a boil and continue to cook until it caramelizes. Do not stir the sugar as it cooks. If it caramelizes unevenly, you can move it around by swirling it in the pan. When the sugar is a rich amber, stir in the remaining 2¾ cups half-and-half all at once. Reduce the heat to low, stirring occasionally, and let the half-and-half warm until all the sugar melts and the mixture is smooth. Using a whisk, gradually stir in the cornstarch mixture. Increase the heat to medium and bring the custard to a boil, stirring constantly with the whisk.

Pour a small amount of the hot custard into the yolks, stirring them briskly as you pour. Gradually add about 1 cup of the hot custard to the yolks, continuing to stir. When you have added enough to warm the yolks, add them to the saucepan and reduce the heat to very low. Cook slowly for about 15 minutes, stirring often, until the custard has thickened noticeably. Do not let the custard boil once the yolks have been added.

With the mixture off the heat, stir in the butter. Pour into the prepared shell. Cover the custard with plastic wrap and refrigerate it until cold, at least 2 hours.

MERINGUE PREPARATION

Preheat the oven to 350 degrees F.

Beat the egg whites until they hold soft peaks. Beat in the sugar, 1 tablespoon at a time, continuing to beat until very stiff but not dry.

Cover the filling with the meringue, smoothing it with the back of a metal spatula. Make sure that the meringue touches the edge of the pie shell all the way around.

Bake until the meringue is golden, about 12 to 15 minutes. Allow the pie to cool on a rack for 1 hour and then refrigerate it until completely cold, at least 1 hour, before serving.

MAKES ONE 10-INCH SINGLE-CRUST PIE.

BOURBON-SPIKED
PECAN PIE

BOURBON-SPIKED PECAN PIE

ART:

Leslie Sapp

Washington, D.C.

Mosaic of glass, nails & sawdust

DARK, RICH AND LOADED with nuts, this recipe is for serious dessert lovers.

Note: Five-inch disposable pie tins are available in supermarkets, and 6-inch shallow ones can be found in specialty kitchenware shops, but you can also bake this filling in a prebaked 9-inch pie shell for 45 to 55 minutes, or until puffed.

1	recipe basic pie dough for one 9-inch double-crust pie shell (page 9) or 1 prebaked 9-inch pie shell (page 9)

Filling

4	large eggs
¾	cup dark corn syrup
¾	cup sugar
6	tablespoons unsalted butter, melted
6	tablespoons bourbon
¼	cup molasses
¼	teaspoon salt
1½	cups coarsely chopped pecans plus 1 cup pecan halves
1	cup heavy cream, whipped, flavored with 2 tablespoons bourbon (optional)

CRUST PREPARATION

Preheat the oven to 425 degrees F.

If making individual pies, divide the dough into 8 pieces. Roll out each piece and fit it into a 5- or 6-inch pie pan. Trim and crimp the edges. Set the scraps of trimmed dough aside. Refrigerate the pie shells for 10 minutes. After the shells are chilled, line each one with aluminum foil and fill with baking weights or dried beans. Bake for about 6 minutes, until the pie shells begin to brown around the edges. Remove the weights and foil and bake an additional 5 to 6 minutes, until lightly browned. After the pie shells have cooled, patch any holes carefully with the dough scraps. Moisten the patches with a little water before pressing them into place. Return the pie shells to the oven for a minute or two to bake the patches.

FILLING PREPARATION

Reduce the oven temperature to 375 degrees F.

Beat together the eggs, corn syrup, sugar, butter, bourbon, molasses and salt. Stir in the chopped pecans.

ASSEMBLY AND BAKING

Spoon the filling into the pie shells, being careful to distribute the chopped pecans evenly. Decorate the tops of the pies with the pecan halves, pressing them into the filling gently. Bake the pies for 20 to 25 minutes, until firm.

Let the pies cool on a rack at least 45 minutes before serving. Slip them out of their pans and decorate the tops with bourbon-flavored whipped cream, if desired.

MAKES 8 SINGLE-CRUST PIES, 5 OR 6 INCHES
IN DIAMETER, OR ONE 9-INCH SINGLE-CRUST PIE.

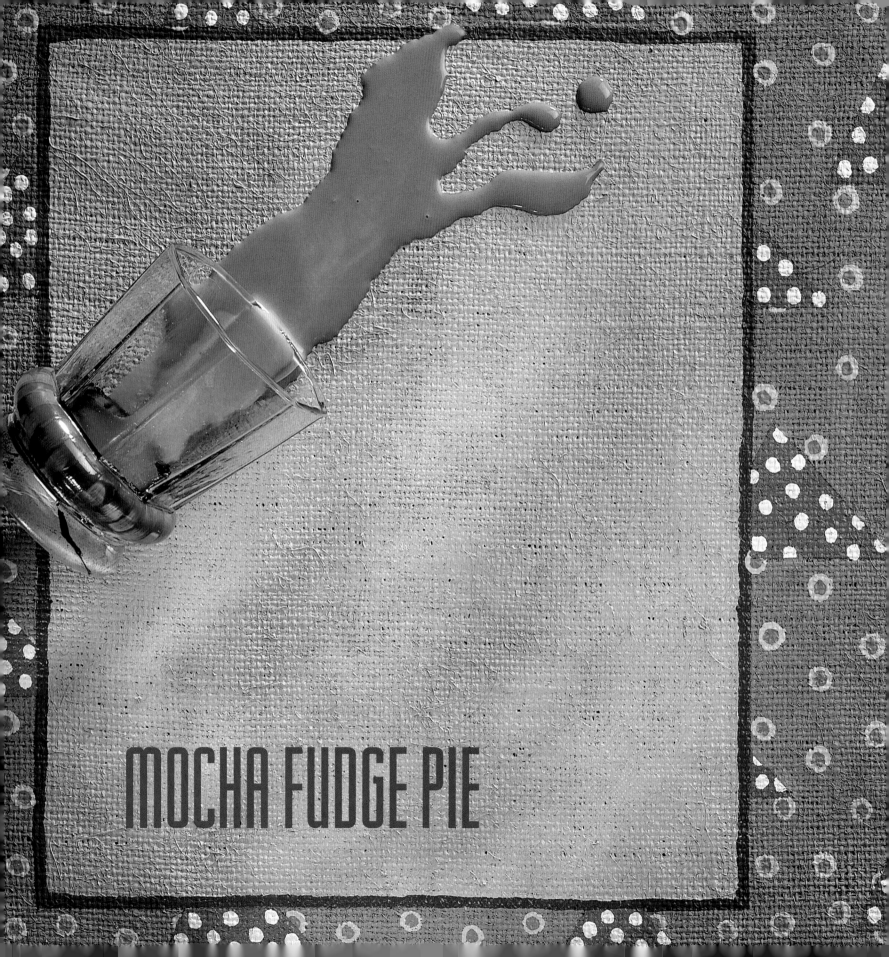

MOCHA FUDGE PIE

MOCHA FUDGE PIE

THIS IS A SOPHISTICATED brownie pie, densely chocolaty and, with the coffee flavor, not too sweet. Bittersweet chocolate is less sweet than semisweet and is critical to the taste, but in a pinch, semisweet can be substituted.

Look for bittersweet chocolate in the candy aisle of the grocery store, at confectioneries or at gourmet grocery stores.

1	prebaked 9-inch pie shell (page 9)
¾	cup unsalted butter
3	ounces bittersweet chocolate
3	large eggs
1	cup sugar
¼	cup all-purpose flour
¼	cup unsweetened cocoa
2	tablespoons instant coffee granules

Powdered sugar and cocoa for dusting (optional)

ART:

Elyse Shalom

Gaithersburg, Maryland

Acrylic on burlap

Prepare the pie shell.

Preheat the oven to 350 degrees F.

In the top of a double boiler, melt butter and chocolate together. Set aside to cool to room temperature.

With an electric mixer, beat together the eggs and sugar on high speed until they are very thick and light, about 5 minutes. On low speed, blend in the flour, cocoa and coffee granules. Stir in the chocolate-butter mixture completely. Pour the filling into the pie shell.

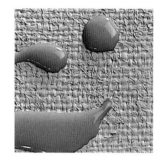

Bake 30 to 35 minutes. The center of the pie will still be moist and slightly soft, while the edge should be firm.

Cool on a rack at least 1 hour before serving.

Just before serving, dust the pie with powdered sugar and/or cocoa, if desired.

MAKES ONE 9-INCH SINGLE-CRUST PIE.

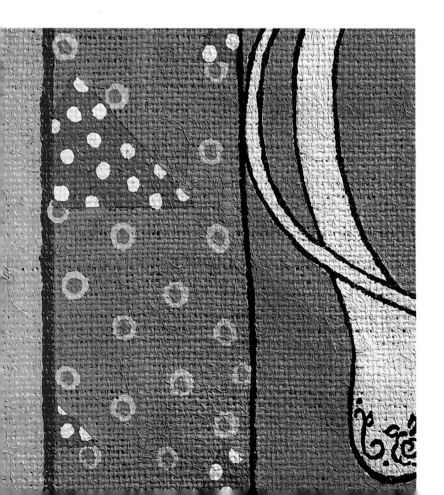

Sour Cherries in
Gewürztraminer Pie

Fresh sour cherries undoubtedly make the best pie, but because they are fragile and hard to store and ship, they are maddeningly hard to come by. Although the United States is the world's primary producer, the majority of sour cherries are destined for cans. Picking your own in June and July is one way to eat your fill; otherwise, look for them in farmers' markets. The cherries in this pie, barely cooked, retain their shape and are still bursting with juice. Kirsch heightens the flavor, and Gewürztraminer wine adds a touch of spice.

1	prebaked 9-inch pie shell (page 9)
5	cups fresh or frozen sour cherries, stems and pits removed, juice reserved (do not use canned)
2	cups Gewürztraminer
¼	cup kirsch (cherry brandy)
1¼	cups sugar
5	teaspoons quick-cooking tapioca
⅛	teaspoon ground cloves

Sour Cherries in Gewürztraminer Pie

ART:

Jody Boozel

Sterling, Virginia

Hand-colored photograph

102

Prepare the pie shell.

In a medium nonaluminum saucepan, stir together the juice drained from the cherries, the Gewürztraminer and the kirsch. Set the pan over medium heat and let the mixture boil until it is reduced to 1 cup. (If the mixture reduces too much, add some cold water to make up the difference.) Refrigerate the syrup until very cold, at least 30 minutes.

Stir the sugar, tapioca and cloves into the cold syrup and set the mixture aside for 30 minutes.

Set the saucepan over medium heat and bring it to a rolling boil, stirring continuously. Let the mixture boil for 1 minute, remove it from the heat and set it aside to cool for 20 minutes. Stir in the cherries. Pour the filling into the prebaked shell and smooth the top with a rubber spatula.

Before serving, cool in the refrigerator for at least 2 hours.

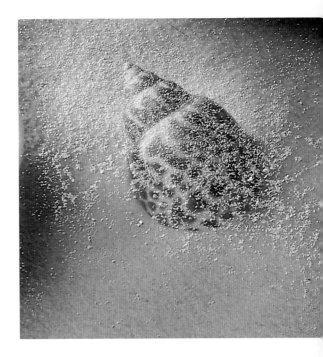

MAKES ONE 9-INCH SINGLE-CRUST PIE.

RICOTTA NUT
CRUNCH PIE

THIS PIE IS A MOSAIC of apricots, chocolate and toasted almonds levitating in lightly sweetened ricotta and whipped cream. The filling requires no baking, but be sure to chill it adequately.

Crust

6	ounces amaretti or other almond cookies (1½ cups crumbs)
4	tablespoons unsalted butter, melted
¼	cup apricot preserves

Filling

½	cup slivered almonds
½	cup ground or finely chopped almonds
2	cups (15 ounces) ricotta cheese
½	cup sugar
1	teaspoon vanilla
½	cup (3 ounces) chopped semisweet chocolate
¼	cup diced dried apricots
1	cup heavy cream

RICOTTA NUT CRUNCH PIE

ART:

Deeda Hull

Takoma Park, Maryland

Watercolor pencil

106

CRUST PREPARATION

Preheat the oven to 400 degrees F.

Crush the cookies into crumbs in a food processor or put them into a plastic bag and crush them with a rolling pin. You will need 1½ cups of crumbs. Put the crumbs and butter into a 9-inch pie pan and use your fingers to mix them together. Press the crumb mixture onto the bottom and sides of the pie pan.

Bake for 6 minutes. Let the crust cool to room temperature and then set it in the refrigerator to chill completely. When the crust is cold, spread the apricot preserves over the bottom of it.

FILLING PREPARATION

While the pie shell is baking, toast the slivered and ground almonds for the filling. Spread them on separate small sheet pans and bake them 5 to 6 minutes, until fragrant and lightly browned.

Puree the ricotta, sugar and vanilla in a food processor until very smooth. (This step is not essential if you do not have a food processor; simply mix the ingredients thoroughly.) Spoon the ricotta mixture into a medium mixing bowl and stir in the chopped chocolate, ground almonds and apricots.

Beat the heavy cream until very stiff and fold it into the ricotta mixture. Spoon the filling into the prepared shell and then create swirls in the top of the pie with the back of the spoon. Sprinkle the toasted slivered almonds over the pie and refrigerate until very cold, at least 3 hours.

MAKES ONE 9-INCH SINGLE-CRUST PIE.

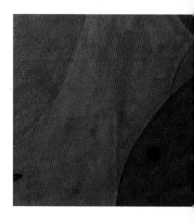

Butter-Brickle Banana Cream Pie

Butter-Brickle Banana Cream Pie

BANANAS ARE SO RICH and smooth that cracked nut brittle is the perfect accent for them. This pie is best served fresh, when the crust is crisp and the butter brickle is crunchy. It is especially good with an all-butter crust.

Prepare the crust, butter brickle and pastry cream in advance, but do not assemble the pie until just before serving.

1	prebaked 10-inch pie shell (page 9)

Butter Brickle

⅓	cup (5⅓ tablespoons) unsalted butter
⅓	cup sugar
⅓	cup (about 1½ ounces) slivered almonds

Pastry Cream

1	quart half-and-half
3	large egg yolks
1	cup sugar
½	cup cornstarch
	Pinch salt
2	tablespoons unsalted butter
½	teaspoon almond extract
2	medium firm-ripe bananas
1	cup heavy cream

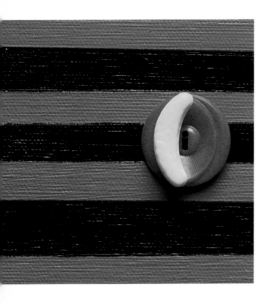

ART:

Groover Cleveland

Washington, D.C.

Acrylic

BUTTER BRICKLE PREPARATION

Lightly oil a 10-inch square piece of foil. Put the butter, sugar and slivered almonds in a medium heavy-bottomed saucepan. Bring the mixture to a boil over medium heat, stirring constantly and rapidly with a wooden spoon. Continue to cook, stirring constantly, until the mixture is light golden brown. (Don't worry if the butter brickle looks a little oily.) Pour it onto the oiled foil and spread until thin. Set aside to cool.

PASTRY CREAM PREPARATION

In a medium mixing bowl, beat together ¼ cup of the half-and-half and the egg yolks and set aside.

In a large heavy-bottomed saucepan, stir together the sugar, cornstarch and salt. Gradually blend in the remaining 3¾ cups half-and-half and bring to a simmer over medium heat. Cook over low heat, stirring constantly, until the mixture is thick and steamy. Remove from the heat and gradually add about 1 cup of the hot half-and-half mixture to the beaten yolks, whisking constantly. Pour the warmed yolk mixture into the saucepan, stirring well. Return the pan to the heat and cook over low heat, stirring constantly, for about 3 minutes. Do not let the pastry cream boil. Remove from heat and stir in the butter and almond extract.

Pour the pastry cream into a mixing bowl and press plastic wrap directly down onto the surface to prevent a skin from forming. Let the pastry cream cool to room temperature and refrigerate until you are ready to assemble the pie. Once the pastry cream has cooled to room temperature, the pie may be assembled whenever you are ready to serve it.

ASSEMBLY

Break the butter brickle into pieces and crush them in a food processor, or put the butter brickle pieces into a plastic bag and crush them with a rolling pin. Sprinkle half the butter brickle in the bottom of the pie shell. Slice the bananas over the butter brickle. Spoon the pastry cream over the bananas and smooth it with a spatula.

Whip the cream until very stiff and pipe it over the pastry cream with a pastry bag. If you have no pastry bag, spread the cream with a spatula. Sprinkle the remaining butter brickle over the top of the pie. Serve immediately.

———————

MAKES ONE 10-INCH SINGLE-CRUST PIE.

Peach Pie, Oklahoma Style

BUTTERY AND COMFORTING, this pie is easy to make, once the peaches are peeled. While your pie is baking, prepare a pitcher of lemony iced tea.

1	prebaked 9-inch pie shell (page 9)
4	large peaches
1	tablespoon cornstarch
¼	cup lemon juice, freshly squeezed (from 1 large lemon)
4	large eggs
½	cup unsalted butter, melted
½	cup sugar
¼	teaspoon salt
1	teaspoon vanilla
¼	cup sugar for sprinkling over pie

Peach Pie, Oklahoma Style

ART:

Laurie McCampbell

Eau Claire, Wisconsin

Colored pencil & watercolor

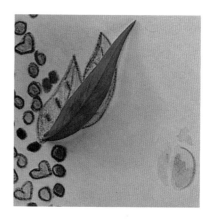

Prepare the pie shell.

Preheat the oven to 350 degrees F.

Bring a large pot of water to a boil and drop in the peaches. After 30 seconds, remove the peaches with a slotted spoon. Let them cool for a minute or two and remove the skins with a small, sharp knife. Pit 3 of the peaches and chop them into ½-inch pieces. Fill the prebaked pie shell with the chopped peaches. Pit the remaining peach and cut it into slices ¼ inch thick. Arrange the slices on top of the chopped peaches.

In a medium mixing bowl, dissolve the cornstarch in the lemon juice. Add the eggs, melted butter, ½ cup sugar, salt and vanilla. Beat until smooth. Slowly pour the custard mixture over the peaches. Sprinkle the remaining ¼ cup sugar over the top of the pie.

Bake for 35 to 40 minutes, or until the pie is firm to the touch and brown on top.

Cool completely on a rack before serving, at least 1 hour.

MAKES ONE 9-INCH SINGLE-CRUST PIE.

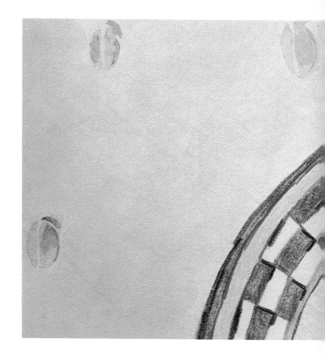

Upside-Down Fried-Pear Pie

INSPIRED BY A RECIPE from Renée's cousin Hélène, this variation on a traditional tarte Tatin is baked in a skillet and served from the pan while still warm. Although traditional tarte Tatin requires some pan-flipping finesse, this version does not. It's great for breakfast, served with a steaming mug of strong coffee.

Crust

1¼	cups all-purpose flour
⅛	teaspoon salt
5	tablespoons very cold, unsalted butter, cut into small pieces
1	large egg yolk
2	tablespoons cold water

Filling

6	firm, ripe Bosc, Bartlett or Anjou pears
¾	cup sugar
3	tablespoons unsalted butter
	Juice from 1 lemon
¼	cup all-purpose flour

Egg Wash

1	large egg yolk, beaten with 1 tablespoon milk

Upside-Down Fried-Pear Pie

ART:

Ed Lawrence

Washington, D.C.

Gouache

CRUST PREPARATION

Put the flour, salt and butter into a medium mixing bowl. Cut the butter into the flour, using a pastry blender, until the pieces of butter are the size of small peas. (This can also be done in a mixer on low speed.) Stir the egg yolk and water together and add them to the flour-butter mixture. Toss with a fork until the dough begins to hold together. Gather the dough together with your hands and knead it gently just until it forms a ball. Press the dough into a flat disk, wrap it in plastic wrap and refrigerate it for 30 minutes.

To roll out the dough, place a 12-inch square of plastic wrap on the counter. Set the disk on the plastic. Cover with another square of plastic wrap. Roll out the dough between the layers of plastic to a circle 10 inches in diameter. Place the dough (still encased in plastic wrap) on a sheet pan and refrigerate it while you make the filling.

FILLING PREPARATION

Preheat the oven to 400 degrees F.

Peel and core the pears and cut them into ½-inch slices or chunks.

Put the sugar, butter and lemon juice into a 10-inch nonaluminum ovenproof skillet and set it over medium heat. Stir the mixture occasionally while it cooks. The butter and sugar will melt and bubble and then caramelize. As soon as the butter and sugar become amber-colored, add the pears. Sprinkle the flour over the pears and toss everything together with a wooden spoon. The caramel may be a little sticky, but it will melt in the oven. Remove from the heat. Smooth the top of the pears with the back of the spoon.

ASSEMBLY AND BAKING

Remove the dough from the refrigerator, peel off the top layer of plastic wrap and trim the edge of the crust with a pastry wheel or a small, sharp knife. Make decorative holes in the crust with small cutters, if desired. Flop the crust over the pears and peel off the second piece of plastic wrap.

Brush the crust with egg wash and bake until the top is crisp, about 25 to 30 minutes. Serve while still hot.

MAKES ONE 10-INCH SINGLE-CRUST PIE.

Cherry Berry Jam Pie

Strawberry Jam Pie

BEST MADE WHEN SWEET local strawberries are available, this pie is as easy to make as a quick batch of strawberry jam. The berries are not cooked, so they remain juicy. Small berries are prettiest, make the pie easier to fill and eat, and tend to be deeper in flavor. This pie is delectable with lots of unsweetened whipped cream.

1	prebaked 9-inch pie shell (page 9)
3	pints fresh strawberries, washed, well drained and hulled
¾	cup sugar
2	tablespoons cornstarch
2	tablespoons lemon juice, freshly squeezed

ART:

P. Dubroof

Rockville, Maryland

Acrylic, paint & oil stick

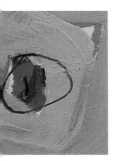

Prepare the pie shell.

Puree 1 pint of the largest berries. Strain the puree and set it aside.

In a medium nonaluminum saucepan, stir together the sugar and cornstarch. Stir in the lemon juice, mixing thoroughly to be sure that there are no lumps. Gradually stir in the strawberry puree. Cook over medium-low heat, stirring constantly, until the mixture reaches a boil. Adjust the heat until the mixture is simmering slowly and cook for 1 minute, stirring constantly.

Mix the puree with the strawberries and spoon the filling into the prebaked pie shell. Chill until firm, about 1 hour.

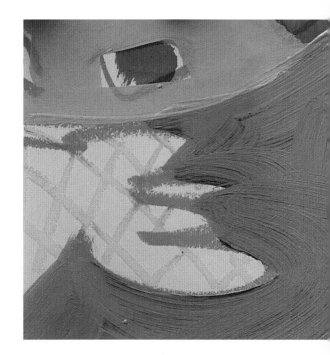

MAKES ONE 9-INCH SINGLE-CRUST PIE.

BLACK
BOTTOM
PIE

BLACK BOTTOM PIE

ART:

Kathy Walters

Washington, D.C.

Colored pencil

126

CARSON GULLEY, dubbed the "dean of chefs" during his Depression-era tenure at the University of Wisconsin, was known as the creator of black bottom pie. His original recipe is still a well-kept secret. My mother claims that this version, which she developed through much trial and error, is an absolutely perfect re-creation. We believe her. Black bottom pie is a tribute to the Dairy State: a chocolate bottom layer is hidden under plenty of velvety-cool egg custard and a mound of softly whipped cream.

Crust

12	zwieback
¼	cup unsalted butter, melted
½	cup semisweet chocolate chips
¼	cup milk

Filling

1	cup sugar
3	tablespoons cornstarch
¼	teaspoon salt
2⅓	cups milk
4	large egg yolks, slightly beaten
2⅓	tablespoons unsalted butter
1¼	teaspoons vanilla
½	cup heavy cream

Topping

½	cup heavy cream
	Semisweet chocolate curls (optional)

CRUST PREPARATION

Preheat the oven to 325 degrees F.

Crush the zwieback into fine crumbs in a food processor or put them into a plastic bag and crush them with a rolling pin. Put the crumbs and the melted butter

into a 9-inch glass pie pan and use your fingers to mix them together. Press the crumb mixture firmly and evenly over the bottom and up the sides of the pie pan. Bake for 5 minutes.

While the crust is baking, melt the chocolate chips with the milk over low heat, stirring until smooth.

Remove the crust from the oven. While it is still hot, spread the chocolate mixture over the bottom. Cool completely.

FILLING PREPARATION

In a medium saucepan, combine the sugar, cornstarch and salt. Gradually stir in the milk. Cook the mixture over low heat, stirring constantly, until thick and smooth. Remove the saucepan from the heat. Slowly add a small amount of the hot custard to the beaten egg yolks while stirring. Add more of the custard slowly, still stirring. Pour the yolk-custard mixture into the custard remaining in the saucepan and mix well. Cook over low heat, stirring continuously, for 3 minutes. Pour the custard into a mixing bowl and stir in the butter and vanilla. Cover the bowl with plastic wrap and refrigerate until cold, at least 2 hours.

When the custard is cold, whip the heavy cream until it is stiff and fold it into the custard. Spoon the filling into the crust, cover with plastic wrap and refrigerate for at least 1 hour.

TOPPING PREPARATION

Just before serving, whip the heavy cream until stiff peaks form and cover the top of the pie with it. Decorate the pie with chocolate curls, if desired.

Tip: To make chocolate curls, you will need 1 ounce of room-temperature semisweet chocolate and a carrot peeler. Working over a plate, gently pull the peeler across the longest edge of the chocolate. Let the curls form naturally and drop onto the plate.

MAKES ONE 9-INCH SINGLE-CRUST PIE.

Tutti-Frutti Pie

As TROPICAL FRUITS gradually find a more prominent place in the produce department, I look for new ways to cook with them. Rich, fleshy mangoes and sweet, syrupy pineapple together make a wonderful pie, spiced with a couple of pinches of cayenne pepper.

Tutti-Frutti Pie

ART:

Paulette Comet

Baltimore, Maryland

Jellybean & paint collage

1	recipe basic pie dough for one 10-inch double-crust pie (page 9)

Filling

2	large firm-ripe mangoes
1	large ripe pineapple
3	tablespoons lime juice, freshly squeezed (from 2 limes)
¾	cup sugar
6	tablespoons all-purpose flour
½	teaspoon ground cinnamon
2	pinches ground cayenne pepper

Egg Wash and Topping

1	large egg yolk, beaten with 1 tablespoon milk
2	teaspoons sugar
¼	teaspoon ground cinnamon

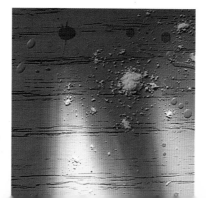

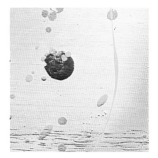

CRUST PREPARATION

Roll out the larger piece of the pie dough and use it to line a 10-inch pie pan. Trim and crimp the edge and refrigerate the pie shell while you prepare the filling.

FILLING PREPARATION

Preheat the oven to 400 degrees F.

With a small, sharp knife, peel the mangoes and slice the flesh off the pit. Cut the flesh into 1-inch chunks. You should have about 2 cups. Put the chunks into a medium mixing bowl. Peel the pineapple and remove the core with a sharp knife. Cut the flesh into 1-inch chunks. You should have about 6 cups. Add the pineapple to the mango. Sprinkle the lime juice over the fruit and toss gently.

In a small bowl, stir together the sugar, flour, cinnamon and cayenne. Add the dry ingredients to the fruit and toss gently, until thoroughly combined.

ASSEMBLY AND BAKING

Spoon the fruit into the pie shell.

Roll out the smaller piece of the dough as thin as possible and cut it into long strips ½ to 1 inch wide. Use the strips to create a lattice top for the pie, trimming them as needed. Brush the lattice and the edge with the egg wash.

In a small bowl, stir together the sugar and cinnamon for the topping and sprinkle over the pie.

Set the pie on a sheet pan and bake the pie for 30 minutes, then reduce the oven temperature to 350 degrees and bake an additional 30 minutes, until nicely browned on top. Cool on a rack for at least 1 hour before serving.

MAKES ONE 10-INCH DOUBLE-CRUST PIE.

RASPBERRY-RHUBARBARA PIE

ALTHOUGH STRAWBERRIES are commonly added to rhubarb pie, I think they sweeten the mix too much. Barbara Stratton, chef/owner of Olive's in New York City, bakes this twist on rhubarb pie. Ruby red and brightly tart, it announces summer.

Rhubarb is abundant in the spring and early summer. Buy plenty because it freezes well. Choose stalks that are firm, red and fresh in appearance. Discard the leaves, which contain poisonous oxalic acid. Wash, dry and trim the stalks, chop them into ½-inch pieces, spread on a sheet pan and freeze. Slide the frozen pieces into a heavy-duty plastic bag, seal tightly and return to the freezer. The rhubarb will keep for up to 4 months.

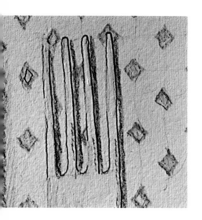

RASPBERRY-RHUBARBARA PIE

ART:

Richard Blackmore

Washington, D.C.

Graphite & colored pencil

| 1 | recipe basic pie dough for one 10-inch double-crust pie (page 9) |

Filling

1	cup sugar or more to taste, up to 1½ cups
¼	cup all-purpose flour
¼	teaspoon salt
3	cups diced (½-inch pieces) fresh raw rhubarb or frozen, slightly thawed
3	cups fresh or frozen, drained raspberries
1	tablespoon unsalted butter, cut into small pieces

Egg Wash

| 1 | large egg yolk, beaten with 1 tablespoon milk |

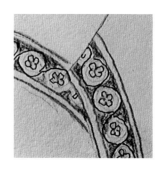

CRUST PREPARATION

Roll out the larger piece of the pie dough and use it to line a 10-inch pie pan. Trim and crimp the edge and refrigerate the pie shell while you make the filling.

FILLING PREPARATION

Preheat the oven to 400 degrees F.

In a large mixing bowl, stir together the sugar, flour and salt. Gently stir in the rhubarb and raspberries.

ASSEMBLY AND BAKING

Spoon the filling into the pie shell.

Dot the top of the filling with the butter pieces.

Roll out the smaller piece of the dough as thin as possible and cut it into long strips ½ inch wide. Use the strips to create a lattice top on the pie, trimming the strips as needed.

Brush the lattice and the edge of the crust with the egg wash.

Set the pie on a sheet pan and bake until golden brown all over and bubbling, about 1 hour. Let cool on a rack for at least 1 hour before serving.

———

MAKES ONE 10-INCH DOUBLE-CRUST PIE.

NUTTY COCONUT CREAM PIE

NUTTY COCONUT CREAM PIE

ART:

Lydia Sarner

Washington, D.C.

Acrylic

I LOVE SWEET AND SALTY flavors together. When I was growing up, my family ate vanilla ice cream often because my dad owned a dairy. He liked his ice cream with saltines. I don't know if he originated this combination, but I have borrowed the idea for this pie. Be sure to use mixed salted nuts without peanuts; the taste of peanuts overwhelms the delicate custard.

Crust

16	saltine crackers
½	cup roasted, salted mixed nuts without peanuts
1	tablespoon sugar
4	tablespoons unsalted butter, melted

Filling

2	large egg yolks
⅓	cup sugar
3½	tablespoons cornstarch
2	cups milk
1¼	cups sweetened shredded coconut
2	tablespoons unsalted butter
1	teaspoon vanilla

Topping

¼	cup sweetened shredded coconut
1	cup heavy cream
¼	cup roasted, salted mixed nuts without peanuts, coarsely chopped

CRUST PREPARATION

Preheat the oven to 400 degrees F.

Put the saltines, nuts and sugar in a food processor or blender. Pulse until the nuts and crackers have been reduced to fine crumbs. Put the crumbs and butter into a 9-inch pie pan and use your hands to mix them together. Press the crumbs onto the bottom and sides of the pan. Bake for 6 to 8 minutes and then set the pie shell aside to cool.

While the crust is baking, toast the ¼ cup coconut for the topping. Spread it on a sheet pan and bake it until lightly browned, about 3 to 4 minutes. Set aside.

FILLING PREPARATION

In a small mixing bowl, beat the egg yolks lightly.

In a medium saucepan, stir together the sugar and the cornstarch. Gradually stir in the milk. Over medium heat, bring the milk mixture to a full boil, stirring constantly with a whisk. Pour a small amount of the hot custard into the yolks, stirring them briskly as you pour. Gradually add about 1 cup of the hot custard to the yolks, continuing to stir. When you have added enough to warm the yolks, pour them back into the saucepan and reduce the heat to very low. Cook slowly for about 5 minutes, stirring often, until the custard has thickened noticeably. Do not let the custard boil once the yolks have been added.

When the mixture is thick and very steamy, remove it from the heat and stir in the coconut, butter and vanilla. Set aside to cool for 30 minutes.

When the filling has cooled to room temperature, pour it into the pie shell. Cover it with plastic wrap and refrigerate the pie for at least 2 hours.

TOPPING AND ASSEMBLY

Just before serving, whip the cream until it holds stiff peaks. Decorate the pie with the whipped cream, the toasted coconut and the chopped nuts.

MAKES ONE 9-INCH SINGLE-CRUST PIE.

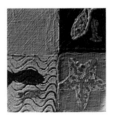

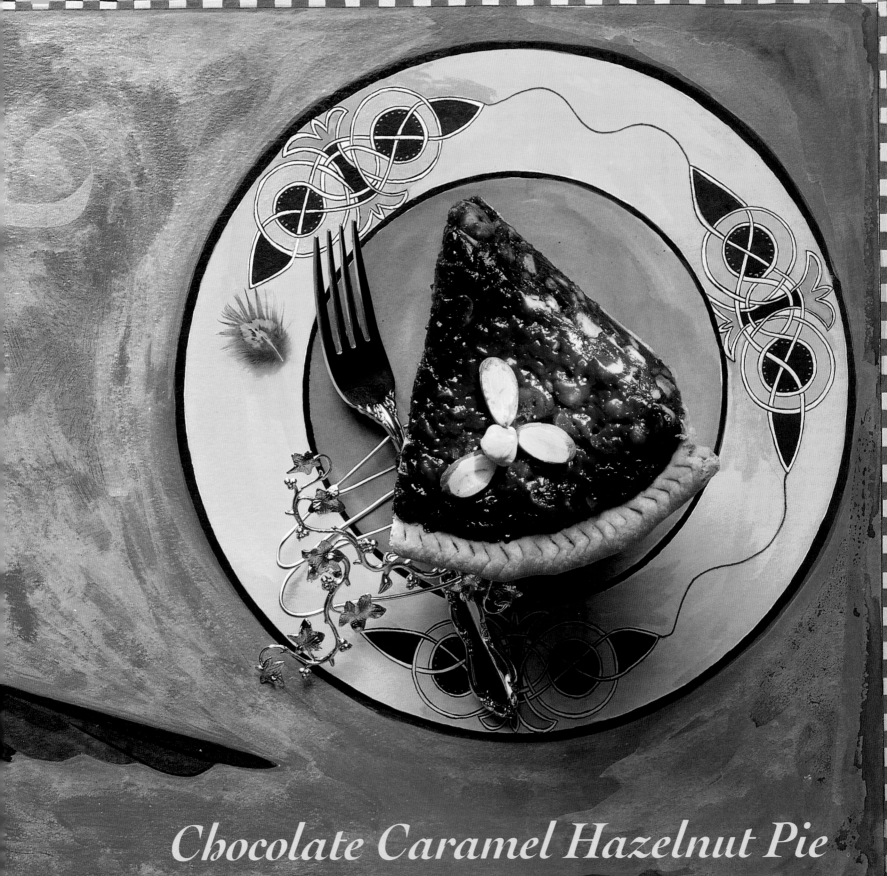

Chocolate Caramel Hazelnut Pie

THIS RICH, NUTTY PIE travels well. Serve it in thin slices. Some people may prefer to use almonds, but the distinct taste of hazelnuts is particularly sumptuous with the caramel and chocolate.

To remove the brown papery skin of hazelnuts, first toast them in a 400-degree-F oven for 5 to 6 minutes, let them cool and rub them in a tea towel.

1	prebaked 9-inch pie shell (page 9)

Filling

1½	cups sugar
½	cup water
½	cup unsalted butter, cut into pieces
1	can (5 ounces) evaporated milk
2	ounces unsweetened chocolate, coarsely chopped
2	cups (6 ounces) hazelnuts or filberts, skinned and coarsely chopped

Decoration

8	whole hazelnuts, skinned (optional)
24	sliced almonds (optional)

Chocolate Caramel Hazelnut Pie

ART:

Maria Cunningham

Silver Spring, Maryland

Mixed media

FILLING PREPARATION

First, prepare the pie shell.

In a large heavy-bottomed saucepan, stir together the sugar and water. Set the saucepan over medium-high heat. Let the sugar come to a boil and continue to cook until it caramelizes. Do not stir the sugar as it cooks. If it caramelizes unevenly, you can move it around by swirling it in the pan. When the sugar is a rich golden brown, remove it from the heat and stir in the butter and evaporated milk gradually, mixing well with a wooden spoon until smooth. Let cool for 5 minutes and stir in the chocolate. Beat with a whisk until very smooth.

Set the filling aside to cool for 10 to 15 minutes and then stir in the nuts.

Meanwhile, preheat the oven to 475 degrees F.

ASSEMBLY, BAKING AND DECORATING

Pour the filling into the pie shell and bake for 10 minutes, until the edge is very brown and the center is bubbling.

Once the pie has cooled to room temperature, about 1 hour, decorate it, if desired, by making small flowers with the whole hazelnuts and sliced almonds.

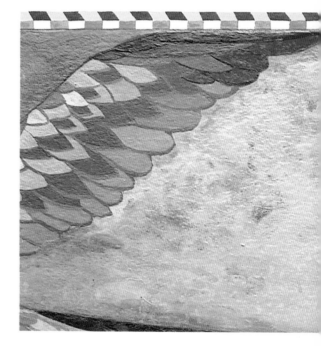

MAKES ONE 9-INCH SINGLE-CRUST PIE.

Tiny Chess Pies

THE EGG-THICKENED CUSTARD of these little pies is faintly flavored with lemon juice and zest. Their name comes from the word "cheese," which was once used generically by British cooks to refer to both eggs and cheese.

Crust

2	cups all-purpose flour
¼	teaspoon salt
⅔	cup very cold, unsalted butter, cut into small pieces
3–4	tablespoons ice water

Filling

2	tablespoons unsalted butter, softened
⅓	cup light brown sugar, firmly packed
¼	cup sugar
¼	teaspoon salt
2	tablespoons all-purpose flour
2	large eggs
1	cup heavy cream
½	tablespoon grated lemon zest
3	tablespoons lemon juice, freshly squeezed

Topping

¼	cup sugar
2	tablespoons water
1	medium lemon
8	candied violets (optional)

ART:

Mara Cherkasky

Providence, Rhode Island

Paper collage

CRUST PREPARATION

Stir the flour and salt together in a medium mixing bowl. Use a pastry blender to cut the butter into the flour until the butter pieces are the size of small peas. This also may be done in an electric mixer on the lowest speed, but be careful not to overmix. Sprinkle the water over the flour-butter mixture. Toss the dough lightly with your fingers until the liquid is evenly distributed. Knead the dough gently until it forms a ball. Flatten the ball until it is about 2 inches thick, wrap it in plastic and refrigerate it for 1 hour.

Once the dough is completely chilled, roll it out on a lightly floured surface until it is ⅛ inch thick. Use a 4-inch round cutter to make 8 dough circles. Using 8 muffin cups, press a circle of dough onto the bottoms and sides of each cup. Refrigerate the dough while you prepare the filling.

FILLING PREPARATION

Preheat the oven to 375 degrees F.

Cream the butter, brown sugar, sugar and salt until fluffy. Stir in the flour and then the eggs, 1 at a time. Stir in the cream, lemon zest and lemon juice and blend thoroughly.

Pour the filling into a pitcher and divide it evenly among the dough-lined muffin cups. Bake until firm, 20 to 25 minutes, or until the pies are lightly browned on top.

TOPPING PREPARATION

The topping can be made while the pies are baking. Put the sugar and water in a small nonaluminum saucepan and bring it to a boil over medium heat. Slice the lemon into 8 thin slices and remove the seeds. Add the lemon to the sugar syrup and let the mixture continue to boil for 5 to 6 more minutes. Gently stir the lemons occasionally as they cook. Remove the slices with a fork, lay them on wax paper and let them cool.

Once the pies have cooled, remove them from the muffin cups. Lay a lemon slice on each one and then decorate them with candied violets, if desired.

Tip: To make grating lemon zest easier, press a piece of wax paper down on a finely perforated grater. Rub the lemon over the paper-covered grater. (The paper will not tear.) Carefully remove the paper and scrape off the zest.

MAKES 8 SINGLE-CRUST PIES,
2 INCHES IN DIAMETER.

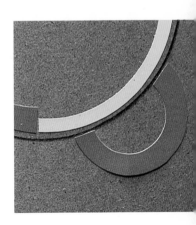

Minnesota Gooseberry Pie

ART:

Gerry Wyche

Washington, D.C.

Acrylic

ALTHOUGH WE ORDINARILY think of gooseberries as green, they grow in a variety of colors, including white, yellow and red. They have a delicious sourness. I rarely see them in grocery stores but look for them at farmers' markets instead. They freeze very nicely if you remove the stems and tails first, freeze the berries in a single layer on a sheet pan and then transfer them to a tightly sealed bag.

Fresh red currants also do beautifully for this pie. Use only fresh or frozen berries; don't be tempted by anything canned.

1	recipe basic pie dough for one 9-inch double-crust pie (page 9)

Filling

4	cups fresh or frozen gooseberries
1½	cups sugar
¼	cup all-purpose flour
2	teaspoons quick-cooking tapioca
½	teaspoon ground cinnamon
¼	teaspoon ground nutmeg
2	teaspoons unsalted butter, cut into small pieces

Glaze

1	tablespoon cold water
2	teaspoons sugar

CRUST PREPARATION

Roll out the larger piece of the pie dough and use it to line a 9-inch pie pan. Trim the edge and refrigerate the pie shell while you prepare the filling.

FILLING PREPARATION

Preheat the oven to 400 degrees F.

With a small, sharp knife or scissors, remove the stems and tails of the gooseberries. In a large mixing bowl, stir together the sugar, flour, tapioca, cinnamon and nutmeg. Add the gooseberries and toss until the dry ingredients are evenly distributed.

ASSEMBLY, GLAZING AND BAKING

Spoon the berries into the pie shell. Dot the filling with the butter pieces.

Roll out the smaller piece of the dough and cut decorative holes in it with a small round cutter. (Use a thimble or small shot glass if you do not have a small cutter.) Cover the pie with the dough. Trim and crimp the edge.

In a small bowl, stir together the cold water and sugar for the glaze. Brush it over the top of the pie.

Set the pie on a sheet pan and bake for 20 minutes. Reduce the oven temperature to 350 degrees and bake for an additional 30 minutes, until brown on top and bubbling around the edges.

Let cool on a rack at least 30 minutes before serving.

MAKES ONE 9-INCH DOUBLE-CRUST PIE.

Brown Sugar Apple Crumb Pie

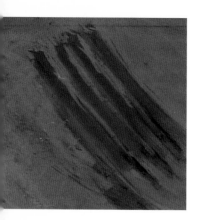

Brown Sugar Apple Crumb Pie

ART:

Mary Connelly

Washington, D.C.

Oil crayon & colored pencil

As EASY AS A COBBLER, this pie is foolproof. The brown sugar not only sweetens it but imparts its own distinctive flavor. Warm any leftover pie for breakfast. It is especially tasty next to a slice of country ham.

Filling

¼	**cup lemon juice, freshly squeezed (from 1 large lemon)**
¼	**cup water**
¼	**cup light brown sugar, firmly packed**
7	**medium Granny Smith, Pippin or other firm, tart apples that will hold their shape when baked**
¼	**cup golden raisins**

Crumb Crust

1¼	**cups all-purpose flour**
½	**cup whole-wheat flour**
¾	**cup light brown sugar, firmly packed**
¼	**teaspoon salt**
½	**cup unsalted butter, cut into small pieces**
1	**large egg yolk**

Topping

1	**tablespoon unsalted butter, cut into small pieces**

FILLING PREPARATION

In a large nonaluminum saucepan, stir together the lemon juice, water and brown sugar. Peel, core and slice the apples. Stir the apples into the lemon-and-sugar mixture. Stir in the raisins. Place the saucepan over medium heat and cook until the apples are tender, about 5 to 6 minutes. Stir them occasionally and gently as they cook.

CRUMB CRUST PREPARATION

Preheat the oven to 350 degrees F.

Thoroughly butter the sides and bottom of a 10-inch pie pan.

In a medium mixing bowl, stir together the all-purpose flour, whole-wheat flour, brown sugar and salt. Use a pastry blender to cut the butter into the dry ingredients until the butter pieces are the size of small peas. This may also be done in an electric mixer on the lowest speed, but be careful not to overmix. Cut the egg yolk into the crumb mixture until it is evenly distributed.

ASSEMBLY AND BAKING

Set aside 1 cup of the crumb mixture. Press the remaining crumb mixture into the bottom and sides of the prepared pie pan.

Spoon the apples into the crumb-lined pan and pat them down lightly. Sprinkle the reserved 1 cup of crumbs over the apples.

Dot the top of the pie with the butter pieces. Bake until bubbling and brown on top, 50 to 55 minutes.

Serve warm or cool.

MAKES ONE 10-INCH DOUBLE-CRUST PIE.

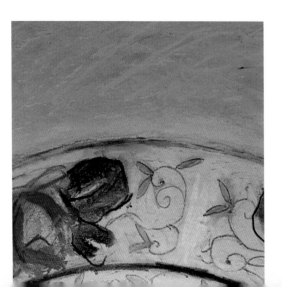

Peppery Sweet Potato Pie

SWEET POTATOES are interchangeable with pumpkin in most pie recipes, but in my opinion, the sweet potato's slightly more dense and smooth texture makes it superlative—perfect for holding up lots of heavy cream. This version is spiked with a little cayenne.

Peppery Sweet Potato Pie

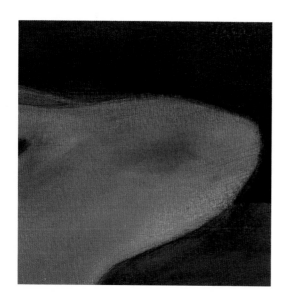

ART:

Donna M. McCullough

Silver Spring, Maryland

Acrylic

1	prebaked 9-inch pie shell (page 9)
1½	cups pureed or thoroughly mashed sweet potato (about 1¼ pounds fresh, weighed before baking, or about 1 pound canned, well drained)
2	cups heavy cream
2	large eggs
¾	cup sugar
½	teaspoon salt
2	teaspoons ground cinnamon
½	teaspoon ground ginger
½	teaspoon ground cloves
⅛	teaspoon ground cayenne pepper

Whipped cream for garnishing (optional)

158

Prepare the pie shell.

Preheat the oven to 425 degrees F.

In a large mixing bowl, beat together until smooth the sweet potato, cream, eggs, sugar, salt, cinnamon, ginger, cloves and cayenne pepper. Pour the filling into the prepared pie shell.

Bake the pie for 10 minutes. Reduce the oven temperature to 325 degrees and bake for an additional 45 minutes, until firm. Test the pie by inserting a table knife into the center. When the knife comes out clean, the pie is done.

Refrigerate for at least 1 hour before serving.

Decorate the pie with whipped cream, if desired.

MAKES ONE 9-INCH SINGLE-CRUST PIE.

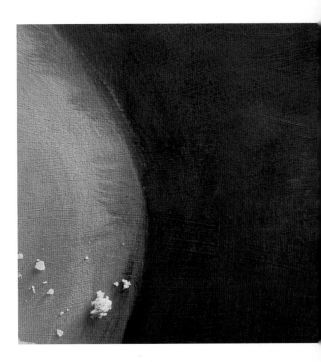